When Textbooks Fall Short

New Ways, New Texts, New Sources of Information in the Content Areas

Nancy T. Walker

Thomas W. Bean

Benita R. Dillard

HEINEMANN
Portsmouth, NH

Heinemann
361 Hanover Street
Portsmouth, NH 03801–3912
www.heinemann.com

Offices and agents throughout the world

The authors and publisher wish to thank those who have generously given permission to reprint borrowed material:

Excerpt from "Triple Read—A Technique for Encouraging Close Reading of Informational Text," an unpublished manuscript by P. D. Pearson. Copyright © 1994 by P. D. Pearson. Reproduced by permission of the author.
Excerpts from *Building Literacy in the Content Areas* by Thomas G. Gunning. Copyright © 2003. Published by Pearson Education, Inc. Reprinted by permission of the publisher.
Excerpt from *Houghton Mifflin English, Grade 7, Student Edition.* Copyright © 2001 by Houghton Mifflin Company. Published by Houghton Mifflin Harcourt Publishing Company. Reprinted by permission of the publisher.

Library of Congress Cataloging-in-Publication Data
Walker, Nancy T.
    When textbooks fall short : new ways, new texts, new sources of information in the content areas / Nancy T. Walker, Thomas W. Bean, and Benita R. Dillard.
        p. cm.
    Includes bibliographical references.
    ISBN-13: 978-0-325-01747-1
    ISBN-10: 0-325-01747-6
    1. Reading—Computer-assisted instruction.   2. Content area reading.
I. Bean, Thomas W.   II. Dillard, Benita R.   III. Title.
LB1050.37.W35 2010
428.4078′5—dc22

                                                                2009046283

Editor: Wendy Murray
Production editor: Patricia Adams
Typesetter: Eisner/Martin Typographics
Cover design: Night and Day Design
Manufacturing: Steve Bernier

Printed in the United States of America on acid-free paper
14 13 12 11 10 VP 1 2 3 4 5

Contents

Acknowledgments

This work, which has now spanned almost eight years, would not have been possible without the help of many people. All of the teachers and students spotlighted in this book are our heroes, and we thank them for their trust and honesty as they allowed us into their classrooms and into their lives as teachers and professionals.

We express our sincere gratitude to executive editor Wendy Murray and developmental editor Jane Harrigan and the staff at Heinemann for their encouragement and guidance as we traveled this journey. Their advice and encouragement unleashed the best of our writing, and we appreciate their dedication to this project.

Finally, this project would not have been possible without the support of our families and friends. They provided many words of wisdom and encouragement along the way as our project grew and culminated with this book. We thank you for being such a beacon of support in our lives.

—Nancy T. Walker
—Thomas W. Bean
—Benita R. Dillard

Introduction

Don't Throw Out the Old, Just Add the New: Expanding the Definitions of Multiple Texts

> *In the young adult novel Code Orange (Cooney 2005), Mitty Blake, a high school biology student, is expected to turn in a term paper with a bibliography that includes at least four physical books. Mitty reacts to the requirement like this:*
>
>> *"Books?" said Mitty, stunned. He was sure this had not been mentioned before. "Mr. Lynch, nobody uses books anymore. They're useless, especially in science. Facts change too fast."*
>> *"Books," repeated Mr. Lynch. "This is to prevent you people from doing a hundred percent of your research online." (1–2)*

We are in the midst of a seismic shift between the bound book and the e-book, YouTube and the evening news, national economies and global economies—this comparison-and-contrast list could go on forever. Caught between the Gutenberg and Google eras, book publishers, newspapers, all print media, find themselves tacking into the wind.

We've seen the power of the Internet in the election of Barack Obama, whose campaign masterfully used it to reach people and unite their efforts on his behalf. We've seen technology's downside in the way interconnected global economies influence one another, taking consumers and investors on a faster-rising and more reckless virtual thrill ride—and falling like the proverbial row of dominoes without any stopgaps.

The use of technology in education has been building for decades, and professional books addressing these new literacies abound. What makes ours different? We capture teachers' forays into new types of texts at a time of transition, when the very definitions of text and literacy are in flux. Many of today's teachers are taking baby steps, experimenting with virtual museums, blogging, and the like in conjunction with core texts. As technology-savvy young adults grow up and become teachers, new literacies will slide into teaching and learning naturally. The teachers of tomorrow will breathe these forms of communication and information sources in ways many of us can't yet grasp.

Yes, we do have amazing schools and classrooms with cutting-edge technology and teachers pushing the envelope. But for every Ning and blog and Skype and Twitter and virtual class trip, there are ten schools that may have one old computer sitting in the corner—and it's rarely turned on. For every teacher who has expertly embedded new literacies into the curriculum to improve students' learning and engagement, there is a lounge full of teachers who are convinced computer-based resources and teaching aren't all they're cracked up to be.

In this book, we meet teachers where they are now and introduce possibilities that don't require thousands of dollars and a rewired building, just a shift in attitude. We show teachers how to go beyond the core textbook and incorporate additional print and nonprint resources in their classrooms. The book is a picture of teaching in action (including artifacts and lessons) that incorporates many and varied forms of text, as well as elements of multimedia, in a variety of middle and high school settings.

The Case for Many and Varied Texts

Every middle and high school teacher has watched too many students struggle with the content-area textbook. Students appear to be engaged yet perform poorly on exams. Teachers who want adolescents to become habitual readers complain because these students cannot comprehend their classroom reading assignments. Like it or not, textbooks still have a stronghold in the classroom, even though some of them may be poorly designed and poorly written. When teachers are required to use these texts, their sense of agency is undermined and many fall into undynamic, textbook-driven routines. We need to rescue these teachers from this impasse.

Professional books, research, and conversations in the field reveal that adolescents are highly literate outside the classroom. They may have little motivation to read textbooks in school but identify with popular media outside the classroom (Lenart et al. 2007; O'Brien 2003). They demonstrate any number of literacies (Moje et al. 2008; O'Brien

1998; Smith and Wilhelm 2002) as they participate in online social networks and blogging sites. They read texts that connect strongly with their emotional lives (Moje et al. 2008). Why can't we provide these types of texts and experiences in our classrooms?

The teachers showcased in this book do. They bring in other sources to complement their core texts, thus counterbalancing the standards movement, which is often seen as narrowing curriculum rather than creating spaces for enriching students' learning (Au 2007). They use technology. They realize that students read texts for different reasons, including interest, motivation, reading level, perspective, and information (Walker et al. 2005; Walker and Bean 2005; Alvermann et al. 2002). These teachers choose text in accordance with their beliefs about teaching and learning. As they introduce new texts into their classroom, they scaffold their instruction so that students acquire a deeper level of learning and experience.

Many contemporary adolescents see books as a kind of historical artifact given the vast array of text available to support inquiry on the Internet. These newer forms of text—instant messaging (IMing), blogging, podcasts, Wikipedia, and other wiki Web pages, ezines (Bean 2006)—coexist with older text forms, expanding students' access to information like never before. Teachers like those featured in this book use various print and nonprint resources to captivate students' interest and increase concept learning. In a nutshell, reading now means shifting between the printed page and computer screens and requires extra teacher guidance.

Exposing students to various ways to express a thought or idea gives them the opportunity to be successful and share their experiences in ways that resonate. The range of options is expanding so quickly that it's not just exciting but intimidating. Which tools will work best for a particular assignment? How should you use them? The important thing is to be true to who you are and bring in a level of "new" that is right for you and build from there.

Expanding the Definition of Texts

Most traditional classrooms, which use a single textbook that is explored through lots of worksheets, limit literacy interactions. O'Brien (1998) notes that "by the time students reach adolescence, their experiences with reading materials and practices in school have taught them to dislike literacy activities" (29). Many of these activities may be the result

When Textbooks Fall Short

of state-mandated standards, which often create a mismatch between student interests and content requirements (Ivey and Broaddus 2001). School literacy that centers on answering questions based on content-area texts (Bean et al. 1999) places adolescents in passive roles.

Slowly but surely, classrooms are shifting from a single textbook toward a more inquiry-based curriculum that includes new ways of defining text (Behrman 2003; New London Group 1996; Shanahan-Hynd 2004; Stahl and Shanahan 2004). Possibilities include "film, CD-ROM, Internet, music, television, magazines, newspapers, and adolescents' own cultural understandings" (O'Brien 2003; Phelps 1998, 2). Texts as defined by Wade and Moje (2000) are "organized networks that people generate or use to make meaning either for themselves or for others" (610).

Expanded definitions of text are consistent with recent efforts to reconceptualize secondary and content-area reading within an adolescent literacy framework that acknowledges multiple literacies (Readence et al. 2004). For example, Behrman (2003) notes:

> Literacy development in secondary schools should not be limited to construction of meaning from a single print text within a content-area classroom, but should involve participation in an array of language activities using multiple texts in varied settings both in and out of school. (3)

Using many kinds of texts in a classroom triggers a different, expanded form of classroom discourse that spans intertextual and critical connections that are quite different from the discourse triggered when considering a single text (Bean 2002; Behrman 2003; Hynd 2002). Students make connections with the movies they watch and the blogs they read and create wiki Web pages to pass along what they've learned. Constructivist and inquiry-based units in science and social studies can be created around primary documents and oral and digital texts (Behrman 2003; Shanahan-Hynd 2004; Stahl and Shanahan 2004). Teachers pull historical examples from the Internet—or from the library—for students to analyze. The point is that the way we provide adolescent instruction needs to shift from a singular approach to a multifaceted, multidimensional approach.

Defining—and Redefining—New Literacies

The term *new literacies* refers to a host of literacy practices that often but not always involve multimedia and the Internet. However, this is fast-shifting territory and scholars like Lankshear and Knobel (2003) note that "new literacies and social practices associated with new technologies are being invented on the street" (31). A general definition of new literacies includes "the skills, strategies, and dispositions necessary to successfully use and adapt to the rapidly changing information and communication technologies and contexts that continuously emerge in our world and influence all areas of our personal and professional lives" (Leu et al. 2004, 1572). Writing blogs, creating podcasts, contributing to wiki Web pages, and reading ezines are the tip of the iceberg in this fast-moving medium (Bean et al. 2008).

In general, studies suggest that reading on the Internet is in many ways more complex than reading traditional print (Coiro and Dobler 2007); the idiosyncratic nature of hypertext presents the reader with a kind of *Alice in Wonderland* labyrinth of navigational choices. Lankshear and Knobel (2007) make the important point that new literacies are not new unless they have both "new technical stuff" and "new ethos stuff" (7). They do not regard simply using new technologies to replicate long-standing literacy practices in contemporary classrooms as new literacies. A central component of new literacies is not "the fact that we can now look up information online . . . but, rather, that they mobilize very different kinds of values and priorities and sensibilities than the literacies we are familiar with" (7). As Lewis (2007) so aptly phrases it, "New technologies afford new practices, but it is the practices themselves, and the local and global contexts within which they are situated, that are central to new literacies" (230).

There is some evidence that contemporary adolescent readers can manage this ill-structured environment quite well if they have prior knowledge about the topic, are familiar with print-based text structures and informational Web-based structures, and know how to use Web-based search engines effectively (Coiro and Dobler 2007). However, Web-based digital terrain, with its idiosyncratic formats, presents special challenges for struggling readers (Wilder and Dressman 2007). Nonetheless, adolescents are native users of technology, and thus they often bring out-of-school experiences with video games and other layered forms of digitized texts with them to the classroom (O'Brien 2007). They are often perfectly poised to capitalize on the creative potential of digitized texts. Indeed, students expect teachers to incorporate many kinds of texts (Internet-based lessons in particular) that involve navigating an array of websites (McNabb 2006).

But new literacies can be used even in classrooms that don't have the luxury of a completely online setting. Kist (2005) visited seven school sites and classrooms in the United States and Canada in which teachers were incorporating creative teaching practices involving new literacies. Kist characterized these classrooms as ones that featured:

- daily work involving varied forms of representation
- explicit discussions of the merits of using certain symbol systems
- teacher modeling demonstrating the use of varying symbols
- collaborative and individual activities
- the sensation of time passing quickly

These important characteristics should guide our thinking as we create lessons that capitalize on adolescents' literacies in and outside school.

Sheridan-Thomas (2007), a teacher-educator working with pre-service teachers, notes, "The concept of multiple literacies is not only about multiple texts or varied text forms. It begins with the multiplicity of cultural identities that are expressed through literacies" (122). Sheridan-Thomas found that preservice teachers who did not explicitly focus on adolescents' multiple literacies conceptualized content literacy as a simple skills-based process.

While taking Sheridan-Thomas's course, these preservice teachers quickly expanded their views of what counts as text, embracing the multiple literacies and multiple texts students actually use both in and out of school. Video games, computers, magazines, newspapers, cell phones, and contemporary television dramas like CSI became the basis for curriculum. For example, a preservice chemistry teacher planned to show selected clips of the most interesting scientific moments from a CSI episode and have students choose one they wanted to explore.

In the Classroom

When teachers solve the curriculum problem in these ways, what happens? Does something change in their teaching? Do students respond differently? Let's step into a classroom and see.

All year in Brenda's ninth-grade English class, sixteen-year-old Prescott, a quiet young man, had struggled with his assignments, not doing most of them. When asked why, he shrugged and said, "They're boring." He told Brenda he didn't like to write essays or create Power-Point presentations. He enjoyed writing poetry.

When Prescott handed in an excellent poem about the injustice he has encountered because he's different, Brenda was excited. She called his home and told Prescott's mother how proud she was of the work he'd done. The boy's mother was thrilled: "He's never earned a grade higher than a D in his life." After that surprise, Brenda received another—an email from Prescott:

> I am glad that you enjoyed my poem. I write lyrics for music and I write poems when I am let down or in a bad mood. It took me 16 years to find out that writing was the best way for me to relieve stress. To me poems turn bad emotions into beautiful artwork. And I know how it feels to be discriminated and let down for being yourself. So I put those feelings of oppression in the black history poem and I guess it came out good because maybe you have felt that feeling before.

How did Prescott, a D student, get inspired to do good work and show enthusiasm? The answer has nothing to do with miracles and everything to do with carefully designed assignments. As part of a thematic unit on the social injustices in black history, Brenda had her students capture—in a poem, an essay, a PowerPoint display, or a posting to a Web message board—an experience related to injustice or oppression that they wanted to pass on to their descendents.

By providing several avenues for expression, Brenda's assignment gave free rein to the creativity of a student who found most schoolwork too boring to bother with. Brenda provided project options students could match to their particular strengths and interests.

Meet the Teachers

The teachers who contributed to this book came to us in a variety of ways. Some responded to our call for volunteers who use many and varied kinds of text in their classroom. Others were recommended by our colleagues or by school principals. Some we stumbled on in our research. All allowed us to observe their classroom teaching for six months. We are grateful for their hospitality and their willingness to be interviewed during their lunch hour and after school. These interviews gave us a deeper understanding of their classroom practices in connection with their beliefs about teaching and of the change that is occurring in adolescent literacy.

All the teachers taught at middle or high schools in the southwestern United States, schools with diverse student populations. Their classes encompassed grades 8–12 economics, history, English, and physical science. Each chose a pseudonym (first name only) to protect their anonymity.

Maria, twenty-nine, is in her second year of teaching eighth-grade physical science. Several students in her class of thirty-five were classified as English language learners. Maria's curriculum is based on investigation and research and included student-generated texts.

Ty, forty-six, is in his second year of teaching ninth-grade social studies. His students all are working below grade level. Ty spends the majority of his time modifying his core textbook and bringing in outside sources to provide different perspectives.

Madeline, twenty-six, is in her third year of teaching eleventh-grade remedial English. She also teaches junior college prep and American literature. She teaches in a portable classroom whose walls are covered with student work. Her prep time is spent photocopying articles from newspapers and magazines in order to capture student interest.

Kenneth, forty-six, is in his twenty-first year of teaching twelfth-grade economics. His teaching experience includes mathematics, using computers, drawing, ceramics, civil and criminal law, government, geography, and United States history. His curriculum comprises simulations that paralleled the course reading.

Phyllis, sixty-two, is in her thirty-first year of teaching eighth-grade English. She has also taught United States history, GATE English, and struggling readers. Phyllis' curriculum includes an interdisciplinary newspaper project with the social studies teacher, as well as thematic units.

Brenda, thirty-two, is in her seventh year of teaching ninth-grade English at an online charter school. The school's students spend four hours once a week in a real classroom. The remainder of their time is spent online submitting assignments and communicating with their teachers. Each teacher's office hours are posted, and students can telephone and email them and/or meet with them in person.

What You'll Find in This Book

Here is what we cover when—enjoy reading it in any order that suits your needs:

- Chapter 1 discusses the instructional tools used in connection with new literacies and introduces examples of the print and nonprint texts used in the remaining chapters.
- Chapter 2 describes how Maria, Kenneth, and Phyllis use varied texts in their classrooms.
- Chapter 3 describes strategies for increasing independent learning.
- Chapter 4 describes using multimedia texts to help students learn concepts.
- Chapter 5 describes using new literacy texts in a virtual high school.

Dig in. We invite you to see where the explosion of new options can take you!

Multimedia, Meet the Mandated Text

Ways to Connect Core Novels and Textbooks to Blogs, Lyrics, and Other Engaging Forums for Learning

In Madeline's junior English class one spring day, a student is telling his classmates about feeling hopelessly different and out of place. He describes how intimidated he felt as a freshman, when he had no friends and everyone else seemed so confident. He walked around campus feeling out of place because of his clothes, especially his shoes. Sitting in class, he realized he wasn't prepared academically. Coming from a small school to a large school was stressful. He spent much of his time playing video games and tended to be a visual learner, but most of his teachers used auditory teaching methods. Most importantly, he felt peer pressure to conform to the high school student stereotype—party and be athletic but don't study. He pinpoints the moment he was jolted out of his passivity: "I was sitting in class and the teacher asked, How do you feel different? *I didn't want to say. I was afraid my friends would think I was too smart. So I looked around and squirmed in my seat and waited for someone else to answer." Other students respond with similar stories from their own lives, and soon the whole class is talking animatedly.*

These students are obviously engaged in this discussion, which, though it might not be apparent at first, was connected to the core novel for this class, John Steinbeck's *Of Mice and Men*. Madeline realized that her students needed to use their prior knowledge as they read to enhance comprehension (Pressley 2000). Therefore, she created a connection between the novel and her students' experiences. Not all seventeen-year-olds can relate to two migrant ranch hands and their challenges in the early part of the twentieth century, but every high school student can relate to the idea of feeling different and out of place.

Madeline asked her students to read "You're Different, How Do You Handle It," an article from *Parade* magazine (a Sunday supplement included in local newspapers nationwide) that had an appropriate reading level and voice for this group. She used this extra reading to make the assigned reading less intimidating. Students wrote short responses to the article, and a discussion began. After the students talked about their own experiences for ten minutes, Madeline segued back to the novel: "Lennie in *Of Mice and Men* has spent his life feeling different. How does he handle it?" Students jumped back into the book, discussing the connections between Lennie's experiences and their own.

This discussion was important for two reasons. First, personal connections deepened the students' understanding of the text. Second, the discussions became a platform for writing. When the discussion slowed, Madeline asked her students to write on the subject of differentness by responding to three questions in their journals:

- How does Lennie handle being different?
- Describe how you handle being different or tell about observing someone who is different. Include details about your experiences or observations.
- What conclusions can you draw about how people handle their differences and the way they are treated by others? Why?

At the end of the period, Madeline announced that she had set up a class blog on which this discussion about feeling different and out of place could continue. She knew some students might feel uncomfortable talking about the topic in class and therefore created a space where her students could communicate their identity and point of view (Kennedy 2003). Students were able to post entries at their leisure in response to statements made by others.

On Friday, Madeline continued the discussion by asking students to examine song lyrics that explore differentness—again reinforcing the theme using material in which the students were very interested.

The students immediately started discussing the latest music with their friends. Madeline ended the week by asking students to find more examples of song lyrics that explore this theme and share them on Monday.

Each year as she teaches the basic required texts for her courses, Madeline looks for new ways to explore the reading and help her students make connections. She knows that bringing in reading material outside the core text can increase student interest. She does this by identifying key themes—differentness in *Of Mice and Men*—and keeping an eye out for material that supports those themes. Madeline reads a lot at home and is always on the lookout for material that will interest her students and solidify the connections she is trying to make in the classroom.

Like all teachers, Madeline maintains a virtual toolbox of teaching materials and approaches. Her teaching materials include a variety of texts, both fiction and expository nonfiction. Madeline explains, "Because my students are functioning below grade level, I believe I should focus on expository text. I feel it's more important for them to read for information, and the students enjoy reading factual material. Therefore I need to find opportunities to incorporate expository text."

Once Madeline has determined the theme(s) of a mandated text, she pulls reading material from a variety of sources—the Internet, newspapers, magazines, anything that applies. After collecting her texts, she determines the reading strategies her students will need to apply to these texts. Each lesson highlights a text and a reading strategy, so that students leave her classroom with a wide repertoire of reading strategies to aid comprehension.

In addition to focusing on the core text, Madeline makes connections with outside texts. During the reading of *Mice and Men,* the conversation of being different segued into genetic engineering. Madeline touched the SMART Board and an article from *Parade* magazine appeared. The students began a rich discussion of parents genetically engineering their children. After several minutes of conversation and the pros and cons of genetic engineering, Madeline dismissed the students to the classroom computers where they completed Internet searches on the topic. The following day, the class divided into two groups where they discussed the pros and cons of the topic. Having access to the Internet allowed the students to research current information in science and ethics and provided a rich discussion in the classroom.

Increasing Engagement

The teachers showcased in this book teach different subjects at different schools, but they all have several things in common. One is that they realize students are motivated by interesting material, whether printed traditionally or disseminated online (Guthrie 2004). To help them find this supplemental material, some teachers administer surveys with questions about students' interests and hobbies. Daily conversation with students also provides insights into what excites and interests them.

In addition to connecting to students, these teachers read widely outside the classroom. Morrison et al. (1999) found that teachers who read in their leisure time bring more literacy practices into their classrooms. They're always on the lookout for interesting material that highlights a theme or instructional objective. High interest leads to high student engagement, and recent research (Bean et al. 2009) shows that teacher creativity can also increase student engagement.

Historically, teachers have focused on the core classroom textbook as the main source of information (Alvermann and Moore 1991), but the teachers highlighted in this book know that varied sources increase the possibility of critical thinking from many perspectives. To help their students refine these skills, they are using new tools to enhance their teaching. Videos and DVDs, once the height of high tech, are now supplemented by MP3s and websites archiving every possible resource. Multimedia tools are a sophisticated GPS system for twenty-first-century teachers who want to increase engagement and comprehension, offering them an infinite number of routes for getting there.

The explosion of multimedia resources hasn't changed the importance of print. Many textbook publishers provide their own supplemental resources, and the list of possible supplements that teachers can find on their own is huge and ever expanding. The following basic categories should get you started:

- novels related to a theme or time period
- nonfiction related to a theme or time period
- environmental print
- maps
- newspapers (stories, photos, opinion columns, political cartoons, maps)

- encyclopedias
- general circulation magazines (*Time, Reader's Digest, National Geographic, Popular Mechanics*)
- specialized and educational magazines (*History for US, Time for Kids, Newsweek for Kids, National Geographic for Kids*)

Here's how to start generating interest in your own lessons.

- Examine your core textbook or novel and consider ways to make text-to-text connections with current information.
- Choose your outside material and determine your discussion points and writing topics.
- Present the supplementary material to your students and have them examine it in relation to the core text.
- Have students predict outcomes to pique their interest.
- Consider using a Venn diagram or another type of graphic organizer to highlight comparisons and contrasts between the texts. (Check out websites like www.edhelper.com
- Have students make connections between the core text, supplemental text, and their personal lives.

Classroom Snapshot

On her interactive whiteboard, Madeline has written the following prompt: *What is your advice for someone who has to or wants to end a relationship?* The question is clearly a hot topic; her eleventh graders are busy writing in their notebooks in preparation for sharing their personal stories. This writing prompt is connected to the play the class is reading, *Cyrano de Bergerac,* a classic love triangle. Earlier Madeline spent time having the students predict the play's outcome. For this particular class, she brings in an excerpt from a *Parade* magazine article titled "The Best and Worst Way to Break Up," in which nine teenagers talk about their experiences. Students immediately begin sharing their own breakup stories. Next, Madeline uses the interactive whiteboard to display quotes from the article and has the students find connections with the novel. As the discussion continues, students acknowledge that they "get" the story. Madeline has used real-life text and her students' experiences to bring to life the love triangle depicted in *Cyrano.*

When she first presents her students with supplemental reading material, Madeline says, some of them feel overwhelmed. "But once we begin discussions and the students see what the article is going to be about, they are a lot more interested. There is a lot more discussion." One example is the opportunity to incorporate articles from local newspapers. Madeline locates an article on the concept of learning to tough it out from a newspaper and brings this into her classroom to launch a discussion. These outside texts provide opportunities for students to connect to their personal experiences. In this example, students write an essay about "toughing it out" and incorporate information from the article and the texts read in class. For Madeline, outside texts are tools to increase engagement through heightened personal interest. "I'm just trying to find a way that reading can be interesting; there are many different purposes for reading. In addition, I need to find ways to interest my students and improve their skills so they can pass the high school exit exam."

Technology impacts learning in a variety of ways. Students are able to utilize skills that go beyond the traditional pen, pencil, and book format. In Brenda's classroom, she uses technology to enhance *To Kill a Mockingbird*. Brenda begins the class by reminding students that they are examining the tone and mood of the novel. After reading several chapters, she instructs the students to create a songfest slideshow presentation that describes the tone and mood of the chapters. Additionally, the slides need to have lyrics to a song and a short essay explaining which chapters the song is describing and why it fits.

In Phyllis' eighth-grade language arts class, the students are midway through a unit on the Civil War, which is also the focus of their current social studies curriculum. Working together, Phyllis and the social studies teacher connect readings in social studies with complementary literature.

Before beginning this unit, Phyllis did her own research on the period, checked out related novels and nonfiction books from the library, and distributed them to groups of students. Each group took notes on their assigned book and answered questions like these:

- Who is this writer?
- What background does this writer have?
- When was the book written?
- Is it authentic?

Phyllis then explained to her students what factors indicate authenticity. After a long discussion about authenticity, Phyllis asked the class to share their book choices with one another and provide proof of authenticity. This way, "Students learn about authenticity and practice making their own choices in outside reading."

As part of a lesson on primary sources, Phyllis used Ann Rinaldi's book *In My Father's House,* the story of a twelve-year-old girl's struggles with her stepfather during the Civil War. "The history teacher is always talking about primary sources, and I want to show them how to determine whether the text is authentic," Phyllis says.

When she introduced *In My Father's House,* Phyllis began by reading aloud from the acknowledgments as her students followed the excerpt on the interactive whiteboard and took notes. She chose this piece of the text so that students could hear the author describe her background. As Phyllis read the introduction, students listed the key statements about Rinaldi's background that supported why she was able to write so realistically about the Civil War. Later, as the students read the book, they took four or five pages of notes on the authenticity of the main character.

Classroom Snapshot

Today Phyllis has the students read an excerpt titled "Emancipation Means Freedom" from Book 6 of A History of Us. She often uses excerpts from this illustrated ten-volume series by Joy Hakim because the books provide voices and perspectives from a variety of sources. "I like the way Hakim set this book up; it's easy enough for the struggling reader," Phyllis says, "while still engaging better readers."

As they read the excerpt, Phyllis has the students complete a sequencing chart so they see the order of events connected to the end of slavery. The students use the chart as a visual support and a tool to check comprehension as they read the novel and other sources on the Civil War. Phyllis also draws students' attention to the political cartoons in A History of Us and asks students to interpret them, both as a supplement to the historical information and as a way of understanding satire. She reminds the class that any of the topics they see in the book could be a good choice for independent research.

Phyllis says, "I have done more with the entire Civil War theme in these two quarters than ever before. The first semester I used fiction writers, but in previous years we have spent a great deal of time on immigrants and nonfiction. I have found true stories that immigrants told and brought them into the classroom. We've also had teachers whose ancestors were immigrants come to class and tell their stories. We use the textbook as a base and find other books with true accounts about real people."

The Civil War theme continues in Phyllis' classroom as the students explore frontier towns and life during that time. At the beginning of class, Phyllis instructs the students to write and perform a skit that takes place in a frontier town. The skit illustrates frontier justice, housing problems, or school life. The skit serves several purposes in the class as it appeals to the artistic talents of the students and allows Phyllis to address literary devices such as dialogue, foil, dialect, soliloquy, and staging notes. Most importantly, Phyllis instructs the students on authenticity by reading articles on town life in that time.

Phyllis believes that interesting material motivates students not just to read more but to understand and remember what they read. Books in the A History of Us series work because they engage the students and encourage them to keep reading. "So often the history textbook doesn't excite the kids," she says. "They read and try to study for the tests. I want kids to make real-life connections. Education is not just studying. Education is going beyond. That is my goal. To wake them up."

New Forms of Texts

Virtual texts play just as important a role as print examples because today's students are exposed to a wide array of technology outside the classroom and are highly literate in this alternative space. Internet resources for K–12 students are growing at an enormous rate. While once it may have been difficult to locate them, there are now a plethora of resources online that make teaching exciting. Students need a large and well-stocked literacy "tool kit" in these times (Kist 2002, 2), and the sites listed below offer opportunities for students to exhibit creativity and demonstrate reading comprehension even if they have limited reading skills.

- www.makebeliefscomix.com/ (how to make comic strips)
- www.acs.ucalgary.ca/~dkbrown/readers.html (readers' theatre)

- www.acs.ucalgary.ca/~dkbrown/discuss.html (children's literature discussion groups for students under eighteen)
- www.field-trips.org/tours/lit/poet/_tourlaunch1.html (virtual tour of different types of poetry)
- www.free-online-novels.com/ (young adult novels by online authors)
- www.classicshorts.com/bib.html (classic short stories)
- www.readprint.com/ (online books, poems, etc.)
- www.learnoutloud.com/Free-Audio-Video/Literature (podcasts of novels, short stories, author interviews, etc.; excellent for students with limited reading skills and for students who travel a lot)
- www.keynews.org/ (news articles for students with limited reading skills)
- www.smic.be/smic5022/ (reading comprehension)
- www.rhlschool.com/reading.htm (reading comprehension)
- www.laflemm.com/RfT/RfTPracticeContents.html (reading comprehension)

Thanks to the widespread use of technology (in various forms) in schools, both teachers and students have access to a wide array of alternative forms of texts. The list of possible supplemental virtual texts is huge and ever expanding. Here are a few examples:

- wiki Web pages
- ezines
- media links (www.Pbs.com, www.pbs.org/wgbh/nova)
- blogs (www.ning.com, www.nicenet.org)
- vlogs (video blogs)
- podcasts
- culture jamming
- www.mediachannel.org
- www.storycenter.org
- iMovie
- clip culture—http://en.wikipedia.org/wiki/Clip_culture
- https://www.adbusters.org
- uncommercials
- www.timeforkids.com/TFK/
- www.pbs.org/wgbh/commandingheights/lo/educators/ ed_u1_gdp_exercise.html
- http://en.wikipedia.org/wiki/History_of_the_United_States

Blogs

Blogs (Web logs) are Web applications that display entries with date and time stamps (Thorne 2008, 436). They can easily be incorporated into the classroom curriculum as another means of communication. Livejournal.com and Blogger.com are just a few online hosts for bloggers. Students can use blog posts as alternatives or complements to their classroom writing assignments. Because blogs are ordered chronologically, students automatically create an archive, making it easy to revise and edit their writing. Blogs also encourage interactive discussion as conversational threads build on one another.

In an attempt to develop blog discussions, Witte (2007) created the Talkback Project, in which her preservice students and middle school students discussed novels online and made many and varied connections to other texts. Along these same lines, several of the teachers in this book mentioned how nightly blog discussions became the basis for class discussions the following day. Ty said, "I get deeper connections and rich personal responses from my students on blogs than would ever happen in my classroom."

Blogging allows Brenda to help students in her online English class communicate their thoughts with her and other students. Brenda uses blog entries as informal writing exercises in which students feel free to voice their opinions on assigned topics and issues explored in their reading. Blogging is also a way for students to connect their experiences with peers' experiences.

Classroom Snapshot

During a unit on women's rights, Brenda posts a picture of women protesting on the classroom blog and includes questions for students to answer:

1. What time period to you think this protest took place (look at the picture)?

2. Why do you think the women in the photo participated in this protest?

3. Why do you think the lady facing the camera is smiling?

4. Do you think discrimination toward women is an important issue? Explain why or why not.

A blog answer must be at least a hundred words in order to receive full credit.

At the end of the week, Benita asks her students to volunteer their blog entry for classroom discussion. A student raises her hand and Brenda calls up the students' entry on the classroom monitor:

> I think this protest took place in the 1960s. I think the women in this photo participated because she was fighting for women's rights. I do not think that the discrimination toward women has been resolved. We are still underestimated, underlooked, and underrated because we are women. We, as women, can do the same exact things as men, if not better.

The Internet

During a lesson on the space shuttle, Phyllis had her students research articles from the Internet in addition to reading newspapers and magazines. Their inquiry focused on whether or not manned space flights during the economic crunch were sensible. She assigned each group an article and they examined it, answering the questions who? what? where? when? why? and how? and presenting a report to the class. The students discovered that people have differing opinions about the scientific research produced by unmanned space flights. The second report explored the continuation of space flights during an economic crunch. As Phyllis explains, "Most kids use the Internet for some kind of research. Sometimes they've read about a book they can't get a copy of and use the Internet to find out the gist of what's in it and whether it's authentic."

In addition to using printed texts in his classroom, Ty uses the Internet to show students how to examine texts online.

Classroom Snapshot

One day in early May, Ty begins his lesson on Archduke Ferdinand by modeling the Cornell method of taking notes. Then he asks students to read the relevant material in their history textbook, use the strategy to take notes, and compare notes with their classmates. After that, using an interactive whiteboard, Ty displays the Wikipedia entry on Archduke Ferdinand, and students compare it with the information in their textbook. One student comments, "Look, the dates are different," which leads to a discussion about credibility of sources. Several students suggest checking other Internet sources. Anticipating this, Ty has bookmarked www.firstworldwar.com, www.eyewitnesstohistory.com, and www.bbc.co.uk/dna/h2g2/A11873900. As students read and discuss the material they find on these sites, Ty makes comments in the margins on the whiteboard. As students point out differences in one or another of the sources, they see firsthand how necessary it is to consult several sources. As the bell rings, Ty asks the students to discuss the implications of the assassination on the class blog in preparation for the next day's class.

Google Docs

Google Docs is a free Web program students can use to create, edit, and store documents, presentations, and spreadsheets online. The program includes a word-processing feature, which is helpful if a student's home computer doesn't have a word-processing program installed. With Google Docs, students can access their files from any computer that has an Internet connection and a full-featured Web browser. They can also see who made specific changes to their documents and when those changes were made. Because the documents are stored online, they won't be lost if a catastrophe strikes a local computer.

Google Docs is a great tool that enables teachers and students to share and collaborate online in real time from geographically different locations. Students can exhibit their creativity, connect their experiences with the assigned material, and demonstrate comprehension. Teachers can use the highlighting tools to target specific material. The program eliminates the use of paper, allows easy collaboration, and encourages revision.

Classroom Snapshot

As a "get to know you" activity, Brenda asks her students to use Google Docs to create a presentation (six to ten slides) about a few of their favorite things. Each slide must contain a picture or other image, along with at least five complete sentences of explanation. Some students take the image requirement a step further and embed YouTube videos. For example, in one slide, a student states that he enjoys playing a particular video game and embeds a YouTube video that explains how to play it. In another presentation, a student explains that she enjoys scuba diving with dolphins and embeds a YouTube video of someone scuba diving.

As Brenda and the other teachers in this chapter illustrated, there are many types of multimedia that can be incorporated into your classroom. In the next chapter, we invite you to see multimedia in play in economics, science, and social studies.

Harnessing the Power of Group-Think

Collaborative Projects for Economics, Science, and Social Studies

This class is fun because we can build projects that we learn about in our physics book.

—Student in Maria's class

Maria's eighth-grade physics classroom buzzes with laughter, energy, and activity. Two students drop marbles onto a five-foot-tall model roller coaster of twisty red and blue plastic tubing, testing their project's angles and curves. They race around the desks in order to watch the marbles slide down the tubing. Detailed diagrams of theme parks, carefully drawn on authentic blueprint paper, decorate the walls. In the far corner of the classroom, lively student videos and multimedia presentations float across computer screens. A girl role-playing an engineer looks at her PowerPoint slides as she prepares her explanation of her theme park's safety features. A public relations person reviews her selling points as a classmate clicks through PowerPoint slides. An architect reviews the blueprints and his argument for the design.

The teachers showcased in this chapter, Maria, Kenneth, and Phyllis, understand that socialization enhances learning. Looking back on their own educational history, they each remember those K–12 classroom experiences that involved projects, group activities, modeling, and a great many outside sources—experiences that were hands-on and interactive.

The classroom snapshots in this chapter highlight instruction that is based on the state standards and centered on the core textbook. However, these teachers break away from the lectures that are so prevalent in content-area classrooms. Instead they use varied texts—many of them examples of the new literacies—and incorporate technology into projects and simulations as they design lessons that grab students' interest and increase engagement and participation. The teachers use traditional and nontraditional texts to enhance students' understanding of concepts in physics, economics, and other content areas.

Why Use Varied Texts?

Some benefits of using varied texts include:

- Connections to their daily lives get students' attention.
- Newspaper and magazines articles are easier to read than textbooks.
- Primary sources are not well represented in many textbooks.
- Textbooks often do not address real-life issues.
- Student-produced texts keep students involved and help them retain material.
- Varied texts allow you to connect disparate content areas, such as economics and literature.
- Varied texts can be integrated with reading strategy lessons.

Classroom Snapshot: The Roller-Coaster Project

In her eighth-grade physics classroom, Maria focuses on core content but is eager to implement more reading and writing strategies. Her class demographic is similar to that in many schools today: thirty-five students of diverse backgrounds, many of them second language learners who struggle with content and language acquisition but are motivated and eager to participate. Because her students struggle with academic language, Maria devises projects to keep them interested. She realizes that learning is enhanced when her students are engaged in the curriculum: "The textbook gets too technical and I want it to be interesting for them."

Preparing for a series of lessons on gravity and motion, Maria searches the Internet for information about roller coasters and discovers a project in which students, in groups of four, each take on a different role as they work together to design a theme park. Since the project involves cooperative learning, provides hands-on experiences, and integrates technology and writing, Maria decides to try it.

As part of the project, students find and examine articles on the Internet about theme parks and roller coasters, determine the accuracy and authenticity of the information, and then design a theme park and construct a model of a roller coaster. In the process they:

- learn and use the Cornell note-taking strategy
- make connections to text
- demonstrate an understanding of vocabulary, including *momentum, gravity, gravitational energy, potential energy, kinetic energy,* and *heat energy*
- apply content vocabulary in their writing
- write a lab report calculating their roller coaster's speed and velocity
- create a multimedia presentation promoting their theme park and the roller coaster's safety features and deliver it to the class

ASSIGNING ROLES

After Maria's students have read the chapter in the physics chapter that introduces the key terms, they form groups of four. Each group has a public relations person, an architect, an engineer, and a researcher. Maria and the students brainstorm the responsibilities of each role and possible personality types. Then Maria makes the big announcement: each group will design a theme park and build a roller coaster. Students immediately begin talking animatedly—this is going to be fun!

Maria also outlines the writing assignment included in the project: lab reports, journal entries logging their progress, and a persuasive essay outlining the safety features of the group's roller coaster. (Maria includes writing in the project because "my students struggle with writing on their state exam and my administration wants them to do more writing.")

Student groups assign roles and set up schedules for using the computers in the classroom, visiting the school library, and completing reading at home. The bell rings, but students are still talking about the assignment as they leave the classroom. This is an excellent sign.

ONE WEEK LATER

Already the project is well underway. Tubing and wooden platforms have appeared in the corners of the classroom. Students hover over architecture paper, sit at computers, or pore over books checked out from the library. Maria encourages students to read the various texts critically, compare their roller-coaster designs with those of actual theme park roller coasters, and be sure they have included the necessary safety elements. Then she says, "Architects, you need to finish your blueprints. Your rough draft of the roller-coaster design is due by Friday. Engineers, researchers, and public relations people, you need the second draft of the essay to me by Friday."

As the students work, Maria moves around the classroom, interacting with the groups and informally observing the level of engagement. Lively discussions take place as students share information and work together. Most of the interactions are harmonious, other than the occasional instance when someone hasn't followed through on the work he or she was supposed to do. One group decides to create a wiki Web page summarizing the information they've collected and post it on the Internet.

To help the students understand and deal with the safety issues, Maria teaches a minilesson (see Figure 2.1) on comparison and contrast.

Figure 2.1   Comparison-and-Contrast Minilesson

1. Present expository text that uses this structure.

2. Highlight the text pattern.

3. Introduce signal words (*although, similar, but, however, different, on the one hand, on the other hand*).

4. Have students create text using these signal words.

5. Integrate a graphic organizer (Venn diagram) into the lesson and have students use the organizer to display information.

(Gunning 2002, p. 329)

She points out the structural elements and signal words and shows students how to use a graphic organizer when comparing several articles on safety.

ANOTHER CLASS MEETING

This class is devoted to the persuasive essay. Students know they need to outline the safety features of their group's roller coaster. Specifically, the designers in each group need to convince the public that their roller coaster is safe. Maria asks the class to identify elements of the persuasive essay and lists them on the board (see Figure 2.2). Then she says, "Today you will peer edit your draft of the persuasive essay. Remember this is a persuasive presentation. You want to convince the panel to choose your theme park and roller-coaster design. Also remember that revising focuses on content and editing focuses on grammar. Please look at one another's papers and then discuss the strengths and weaknesses of the essays." Maria moves from group to group, monitoring progress and offering suggestions. When most students have finished, the class examines some published persuasive essays together. The groups then spend the remaining class time polishing their essays as Maria monitors progress.

THE BIG DAY

The excitement is apparent. Architectural blueprints hang on the classroom walls, a proud display of the students' hard work. There's a five-foot-tall roller-coaster model in each corner of the room, red and

---

Figure 2.2   What Makes a Great Persuasive Essay?

1. State your goal clearly.
2. Include at least 3 strong reasons that support that goal.
3. Support each reason with facts or examples.
4. Anticipate objections and answer them.
5. Arrange reasons in most persuasive order.
6. Use persuasive but polite language.
7. End by summarizing reasons and calling your audience to action.

(Houghton Mifflin English, 2001, p. 436)

blue tubing twisted and curved to resemble roller-coaster tracks. Students huddle in groups, sending marbles down the tracks on test runs.

Maria takes note of how much the students have learned—not just about important physics concepts like momentum, gravity, potential energy, and kinetic energy, but also about Internet research, project design, persuasive writing, and oral presentation. Students have conducted Internet research, taken notes, created charts and diagrams, used the comparison-and-contrast strategy, written essays, and designed and built a roller coaster.

Varied texts, including information found on the Internet, have been everywhere apparent. Maria knows that her students need meta-cognitive strategies to handle the textbook and supplemental texts, and interesting reading gives them an incentive to learn and apply these strategies. "The articles are pretty good, and they did a better job than the textbook. The textbook gets too technical, and I wanted it to be more interesting for them. Designing a roller coaster allows them to make immediate connections to the terminology." Maria especially wanted to help her students get better at reading expository texts. "In the lower classes they are not readers and they are not going to take the time to read the articles. I wanted to make sure they were able to read and use different forms of text."

Besides giving students the opportunity to build a model of a roller coaster, this project, by asking them to search the Internet for resources to support their proposals, has developed their comprehension skills. As Alvermann (2008) states, "Many young people growing up in a digital world will find their own reasons for becoming literate . . . so it is important to remain open to changes in subject matter learning that will invite and extend the literacy practices they already possess and value" (16). While Maria supports the standards and district textbook, she realizes her students need alternative texts in a hands-on setting to support engagement.

Here's how to get started on a classroom project of your own:

1. Search the Internet for ideas for a project-based experience that can help you deliver your curriculum. (One possibility: have your students build a bridge using physics concepts. The PBS/NOVA website has resources and activities; go to www.pbs.org/wgbh/nova/teachers/activities/2416_bridge.html.)

2. Take your time developing and describing the project.

3. Consider ways to integrate reading/writing strategies into the unit.

4. Encourage group work.

Classroom Snapshot: An Economics Simulation

Kenneth uses a variety of instructional techniques and reading material in his eleventh- and twelfth-grade economics courses, which focus on concepts like opportunity cost and demand. Rarely is the core textbook open on students' desks; they read it at home. The textbook doesn't ask students to apply their understanding of economics to real, day-to-day decisions. Kenneth saves his valuable instructional time for simulations and analyses of outside reading material. These simulations especially rely on excerpts from major newspapers.

Kenneth's motto is, "I am not the fountain of all wisdom." Many and varied texts, used *actively*—in connection with conversation, group work, projects with concrete goals—encourage students not just to connect with but to remember the course material. "I try to give them a number of ways to acquire the concepts. When I give them a test, I ask them to think back to the simulations in order to respond to the questions. They might remember something that came up in a class discussion. If they can read it, hear it, and do it, it seems to stick with them."

Kenneth doesn't merely lecture or deliver information, because he knows that simulating an economic process encourages analysis and reflection; he believes students acquire knowledge through hands-on experience. His simulations encourage students to make tough decisions about resources and use economic principles to support their thinking. Simulations can benefit teachers across the content areas by helping students connect more deeply with the course material, both during a unit and during assessment.

During a simulation, Kenneth's students:

- increase their comprehension of the key concept
- apply the concept to a real situation
- read and discuss many and varied texts
- analyze these texts for different perspectives
- use social skills to negotiate the texts with their classmates

Kenneth believes his simulations are an important reason his students are so successful at mastering the material. Let's watch him put his ideas to work.

BOOKMAKING SIMULATION

The following project is a simulation highlighting capital resources, natural resources, and human resources. This six-step project uses paper money and cards representing the various resources, and the students participate in a bookmaking simulation to understand economic scarcity. While completing it, students read current newspaper articles and Internet sources, as well as the textbook. The six steps are shown here:

Steps in the Bookmaking Simulation

Round 1

The students operate as a cottage industry, producing individual books that are all different.

Round 2

Students leave the cottage industry and go into the factory, where they standardize raw materials so that the books are made more quickly but all look alike.

Round 3

Students begin to divide their labor and take on specialized jobs.

Round 4

Problems begin. Students realize that they do not have enough capital goods. If they could buy more pens, the process would go faster and they could invest in more capital goods.

Round 5

The government intervenes, telling the factories that excess product is slowing the bookmaking process.

Round 6

Factories hire and fire workers as demand increases and decreases.

Kenneth begins the lesson by explaining that people encounter basic economic problems such as scarcity. ("I want students to experience what it is like to want more, more, and more when the resources stay the same," he explains.) He directs students' attention to a newspaper article displayed in enlarged type on the whiteboard. The article notes how the industrial revolution ignited a corresponding growth in productivity. Then he introduces an activity for calculating productivity:

> On Friday I showed you how to make a book and I said there were some requirements, right? Each book needs sixteen pages and has to be bound. You can give it whatever title you want. Now we are going to go back to your sophomore year, way back in the Stone Age. Remember that before the industrial revolution there were cottage industries, where each family produced their own necessities. There was no standardized productivity. Okay, make your books using scratch paper.

The finished products are three-by-five-inch books made out of construction paper, each with a different title. While the product is simple, the message is clear. Students have demonstrated their understanding of the economic principle of productivity.

Classroom Snapshot: An Interdisciplinary Newspaper

There are many possibilities for incorporating varied texts into the curriculum. Maria and Phyllis have the students in their classes jointly produce an interdisciplinary newspaper that incorporates writing related to physics, language arts, and social studies. Each class researches a particular topic using a variety of sources, including the Internet, Google, newspapers, periodicals, and the school library. Students are expected to form opinions on a particular issue by finding and evaluating material representing various perspectives. In Maria's class, students are researching the potential of stem cell research and magnet-sustained train systems while students in Phyllis' class examine the productivity of the Supreme Court. Each teacher has a particular method for incorporating writing into the curriculum. Maria has the students in her physics class write summaries of their research articles and convert them into newspaper editorials:

> One of our problem areas in our school test scores is writing. So the administration has asked us to incorporate more writing. I

feel I do a good amount of writing because they do lab reports for me, but I wanted them to do a lot more writing. I now incorporate daily journals and essays in addition to the newspaper articles.

The contributions Phyllis' language arts students make to the newspaper all deal with the federal judicial system and the Supreme Court. She has them form groups; each group will read a variety of materials on this subject. "I want you to gain different perspectives about our government by analyzing texts that have opposing perspectives. To do this, you need to read two different types of texts at the same time. One book needs to be a primary source (written during that time); the second should be a book written today that depicts or discusses the judicial system."

Phyllis' goals for this project are that students will:

1. conduct research using the Internet and the school library

2. distinguish between fact and opinion

3. read and analyze text from different perspectives

4. acquire effective summarizing techniques

The students progress through four phases in creating the newspaper.

PHASE 1

Students gather information from a variety of sources. In addition to the school library and their local public libraries, they find information on the Internet. After the material has been gathered, Phyllis teaches her students how to determine whether it's authentic. Pulling up an Internet article on an interactive whiteboard, she presents a minilesson on judging sources using the writer's acknowledgments, information on the writer's background, the issues discussed in the book, and the year of publication. See Figure 2.3 for a minilesson on judging sources.

PHASE 2

To jump-start the class, Phyllis posts the following prompt on the interactive whiteboard: *In your groups, write a skit depicting a famous Supreme Court case. Use your resources for factual information.* The students immediately begin writing, frequently checking their sources.

Figure 2.3   Minilesson on Judging Sources

1. Is the source up to date?

2. Who is the author?

3. Is the author an expert?

4. Is the author unbiased?

5. Is the writing fair or does it appear to be slanted?

6. Does the author give proof for all conclusions?

(Gunning 2002, pp. 356–57)

PHASE 3

Once they've written the skit, the students perform it. Folding doors between the two classrooms are pushed open. A stage is created at one end, and the audience sits in desks positioned to face it. The actors take their places. The lights dim and come back up on the mid-nineteenth century.

PHASE 4

In the final phase, each student writes a formal article on a famous Supreme Court decision. They use the Internet to find related supporting material to be included in the newspaper article. Phyllis presents a minilesson on how to summarize (see Figure 2.4).

You can carry out your own interdisciplinary newspaper project by:

1. having your students read a core novel or nonfiction text about a particular period

2. researching supplemental texts that address the history of that time

3. integrating research skills into daily lessons

4. instructing students how to examine varied texts from different perspectives in order to determine authenticity

Figure 2.4   Minilesson on Summarizing

Triple Read

1. Read the passage, identifying the main idea in each paragraph and writing it in the margin.

2. Reread the passage, underlining the key details that support the main idea in each paragraph.

3. Reread the passage, organizing the information into an outline.

4. Write a summary of the passage.

(Pearson 1985b)

Additional Resources to Try

Roller Coaster Project Information

- homepage.mac.com/cbakken/physlab/plab99/labs/nmorley/ rollercoaster.htm
- www.angelfire.com/on2/thrillsandchills/
- Roller Coaster Corporation of America: www.rcca.com/
- Roller coaster designers: www.coasters.net/designers/
- American roller coaster enthusiasts: www.aceonline.org/
- General reference website: www.learner.org/exhibits/ parkphysics/coaster.html

Riding the Online Wave

Study Strategies That Help Students Keep Their Balance with Independent Learning

This is a digital high school. With a SMART Board at my fingertips, as soon as students ask questions we can access the Internet. "Let's see if we can find it."

—Ty

Ty teaches in a southern California school whose student body is predominantly Latino. His social studies students have a wealth of resources because he takes the time to develop supplemental learning packets, integrate technology elements into the curriculum, and enact a philosophy of teaching that goes beyond merely transmitting information. Ty is an experienced high school social studies teacher with a philosophy of teaching struggling adolescent readers that relies heavily on scaffolding and guiding their text comprehension rather than letting them sink or swim. Before you read the vignette from Ty's classroom, consider the three anticipation-reaction statements (statements you support or disagree with before looking at a classroom vignette, text passage, video, or other learning material—Bean et al. 2008) that follow (we'll reconsider these statements later):

Read the following statements and decide whether you agree or disagree with each one. Place a (+) for agree or a (–) for disagree on the line before each statement and indicate why you feel this way.

_____ 1. You can never provide too much text scaffolding and guidance for students.

Why?

_____ 2. Students will read and study texts independently using the strategies you show them.

Why?

_____ 3. It's difficult to learn how to use study strategies independently.

Why?

Teaching Social Studies with Varied Texts

Because Ty's ninth graders are struggling readers (third- to sixth-grade level), he photocopies preselected pages of text and annotates them with marginal explanations or questions. In addition, students are able to use iPods with iTalk microphones to record Ty's brief lectures and then transcribe the recordings into notes on their laptops using the verbatim split page procedure (VSSP; Bean et al. 2008). VSSP notes have a vertical line dividing the paper into a one-third column (on the left) and a two-thirds column (on the right). Students record their notes on the left side and reorganize and expand the notes (using an outline, graphic organizer, or semantic map) on the right side. Additional material from the learning packets Ty supplies can be included here, along with questions students have about the topic. Ty initially models VSSP for his students, entering the information verbatim on the left third of the page and showing them how to elaborate on this information on the right two-thirds of the page. (Note-taking systems like this one are well supported in the research literature on content-area comprehension and independent study strategies—Faber et al. 2000; Fisher et al. 2009.) Figure 3.1 is an example of a VSSP note page about the onset of WWI.

Start of WWI

Nationalism

- means deep devotion to one's nation
- European nations (Germany, Austria-Hungary, Great Britain, Russia, Italy, and France) compete & disagree
- disagreed over territory (Balkans)

Acts of Terrorism

- kidnappings, bombings, hijackings, murder
- the assassination of Astro-Hungarian leader Archduke Franz Ferdinand
- today: 9/11, roadside bombings in Iraq, etc.

Sovereignty

- means the right to self-govern
- Serbia's sovereignty is lost
- Russia backs Serbia against Germany
- tied to Germany, Austria declares war on Russia

Let's listen in as Ty begins the class:

TY: Today we are going to start a section on World War I. The last few months, we have looked at imperialism in Asia, Africa, and South America. Now we are entering into the 1900s. We have seen land grabs on the continents as European nations took over Africa and the Middle East and wielded economic, religious, and political power over the native people. Some people may say the world is getting smaller. What does that mean?

S1: Too crowded.

S2: Industrial technology is high technology. More and more technology.

TY: The world is getting smaller. How?

S3: Phone.

TY: Phone, telegraph, mail, people traveling. Countries are doing business. We are now going to watch two minutes of a PBS video, *The Great War and the Shaping of the 20th Century.*

When Textbooks Fall Short

s2: Do we have to watch it?

TY: Yeah. At least listen to it.

Following the video excerpt, Ty reads a passage from *1914–18: The Great War and the Shaping of the 20th Century* (Winter and Baggett 1996). Ty has highlighted this passage in advance, isolating a key statement pointing to unprecedented growth in European populations and in industrial power: "Cities mushroomed: Berlin turned from a sleepy provincial capital of 600,000 in 1870 to a metropolis of 2 million in 1910" (210). Ty says, "Grabbing and colonization are themes throughout history."

Ty has used three forms of text—a lecture, a video excerpt, and a brief text passage—all centered on the rise of nations, industry, and colonization. Like many social studies teachers, he tries to get his students to question the truth of assertions in the various texts they read. He works hard to convey an impression that reading history is more than simply digesting one factoid after another. Rather, by incorporating various kinds of text and different points of view and scaffolding students' reading and discussion with critical questions, Ty is explicitly teaching his students how to read texts (Shanahan and Shanahan 2008).

Ty also:

- brings in texts from the library to supplement the main text
- brings in pictures related to the topic under discussion
- embeds study guide questions in the margins of these texts to jog students' thinking
- highlights key text areas as a study strategy model
- writes clarifying points on texts displayed on the SMART Board
- reads from a library book to supplement a lecture
- uses multimedia material to expand students' comprehension
  - PBS videos
  - newspapers
  - newsmagazines
  - pop culture magazines
  - Internet searches related to course topics (using the SMART Board or students' laptops)
  - podcasts on historical topics

Numerous maps of key countries are posted on the walls of Ty's classroom (and more can be found on the Internet). *National Geographic* is a mainstay in Ty's social studies class. Because this class of struggling readers needs extra scaffolding and support, he has developed a packet of material modified to make concepts clear. The packet cover is a copy of a photo depicting soldiers on horseback at the onset of WWI. Included are copies of pages from the textbook that refer to key concepts that he has defined in marginal notes. For example, the textbook section entitled "The Steady Rise of Nationalism" embeds the definition of nationalism in the text, but Ty includes it as a marginal note: *deep devotion to one's nation.* Where the text refers to *sovereignty*, Ty asks in the margin, *What is sovereignty?*

Other modifications include a study guide with provocative questions on Hitler and Germany (*Why did people turn to Hitler? Was Hitler a good leader? Do you think a leader like Hitler could rise to power today?*). Each of these questions relates directly to information supplied in the textbook but also gets students thinking beyond the text.

Ty also deliberately peppers his lectures and discussions with connections between history and current events and conflicts, including terrorism and America's wars in Afghanistan and Iraq, so students see history as one arcing continuum. On any given day, he looks for ways to connect the subject to students' experiences. For example:

TY: Where were you on 9/11?

S1: School.

TY: The news came on radio and TV. But a hundred years ago, seventy-five years ago, even fifty years ago, we wouldn't have known about this immediately.

S2: For real?

TY: For real, because they didn't have the technology then.

After going over the text packet he has prepared for students, Ty foreshadows the next part of the unit: "We will stop here. So our assignment is the question, *What lit the fuse of war?* Make sure you fill out a cover sheet."

Ty's assessments are based on the learning packets he develops; students use this resource material to answer questions. "For my tests, students can go to my handouts. I don't do any testing without giving students a source. To me education is as much about knowing where to find the answer as it is knowing the answer."

Because Ty sees lectures ("transmission teaching") as ineffectual, he takes a very different pathway, using varied texts and guided comprehension instruction: "I wasn't happy with what I was given to teach with. It wasn't providing enough information to the students. I think they are definitely capable of handling a lot more than what this textbook provides."

Modifying Content and Topic to Engage Students' Funds of Knowledge

Ty's teaching is an excellent example of how to incorporate multiple texts with an eye toward carefully scaffolding struggling readers' comprehension. He is also sensitive to tapping their local and cultural funds of knowledge. For example, most of his students are Latino, but the textbook doesn't deal with the Mexican Revolution. He includes this topic in his curriculum because he knows it is historically important and will resonate with his students: "I asked students if they wanted to study the Mexican Revolution, and they said yes. Mexico borders us. It has a huge influence on this part of the country. No one said, *Why do we have to do this?*"

Ty's unit on the Mexican Revolution contains many of the same varied types of texts that the WWI unit does. During the unit, students create PowerPoint presentations on key figures that intrigue them (Pancho Villa, for example). They continue to practice the VSSP note-taking system to isolate basic concepts. Figure 3.2 shows the notes Julia Ruiz developed based on her text reading, Ty's marginal notations, and her Internet search for information about Pancho Villa.

Additional Study Strategies to Try

One of the key principles of studying is organization (Bean et al. 2008). A number of proven visual strategies can help students see the overall structure of a passage and identify key concepts, including graphic organizers, Venn diagrams, and a fish skeleton–like "herringbone" diagram that captures the five W's of writing (who, what, when, where, and why).

Porfirio Diaz
- in 1876 he was a powerful general against French rule of Mexico (5 years)
- kicked out Benito Juarez as presidente
- hated by people who remained poor

Francisco Madero
- early 1900s
- believed in democracy but was sent away to U.S.
- wanted revolution against Diaz

Francisco "Pancho" Villa
- helped lead the revolution in the north of Mexico
- cowboy who robbed the rich to help the poor
- I found a song about him online at cowpie.com; it's called "Poncho and Lefty" and was written by Townes Van Zandt, but I know Willie Nelson plays it too
- I want to do an iMovie clip of me singing it with Paul Valerio in our class. He plays guitar. I like the chorus: "All the Federales say, they could have had him any day. They only let him slip away out of kindness I suppose."

Emiliano Zapata
- helped the revolution in the south and in 1911 Diaz was out as Presidente
- when I went to San Antonio, Texas to visit my cousins we ate breakfast at a place called "Mi Tierra" that sold "Viva Zapata" tee-shirts. They are very cool and I have one I can wear next week when we do our presentations. I really like this unit!

Graphic Organizers

Graphic organizers show the big ideas and supporting details through a simple system of branching lines. For example, in the unit on the Mexican Revolution, Ty's students completed graphic organizers that chronologically displayed the key figures influencing the revolt against Spain and the United States (see the example in Figure 3.3).

A good way to introduce a graphic organizer is to create a partially completed one with the lower-level details left blank. For struggling

Figure 3.3   Student Graphic Organizer: The Mexican Revolution's Leaders

Santa Anna (1829) vs. Spain	Benito Juarez (1850) vs. France	Porfirio Diaz (1876–1911) defeats France	Francisco Madero (1911) Mexico's President	Victorino Huerta (1911) next President, fought against Pancho Villa and Zapata

readers, indicate where the information needed to complete the organizer is located (e.g., text and page number). Once students grasp how these organizers work, they can begin locating the needed information independently.

VENN DIAGRAMS

Venn diagrams are especially good for comparing and contrasting historical figures or events or varying opinions about an issue. For example, Figure 3.4 is a Venn diagram comparing and contrasting two striking leaders of the Mexican Revolution, Pancho Villa and Emiliano

Figure 3.4   Venn Diagram Comparing Pancho Villa and Emiliano Zapata

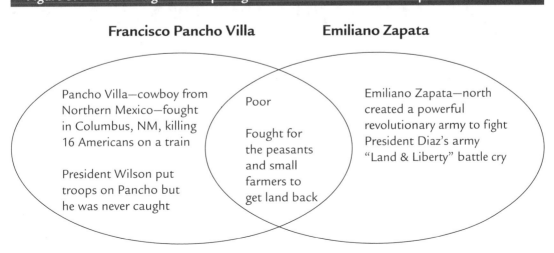

Francisco Pancho Villa   **Emiliano Zapata**

Pancho Villa—cowboy from Northern Mexico—fought in Columbus, NM, killing 16 Americans on a train

President Wilson put troops on Pancho but he was never caught

Poor

Fought for the peasants and small farmers to get land back

Emiliano Zapata—north created a powerful revolutionary army to fight President Diaz's army "Land & Liberty" battle cry

Zapata. Many software programs contain templates for Venn diagrams (Inspiration is one), or students can draw their own intersecting circles. As more elements are introduced, more circles are added.

Herringbone Diagrams

A herringbone diagram is a kind of "fish skeleton" with each branch carrying one of the five labels *Who? What? When? Where? Why?* It is a very concrete way to depict the key information in an article, text passage, or historical narrative. See Figure 3.5 for an example.

Searching the Internet

In addition to these useful textbook and traditional print-based strategies, Ty also provides scaffolding and guidance regarding Internet searches as well, since recent research suggests that while students may appear to be skilled at searching and navigating the Internet (Facebook, Myspace, YouTube, and iTunes, for example), they can become sidetracked by seductive advertisements and pop-ups, ultimately getting mired in navigational detours.

For example, Wilder and Dressman (2006) observed a group of ninth-grade geography students searching the Internet for information on Aruba. Struggling readers were typically overwhelmed by the sheer volume of sites a typical Google search reveals. They often chose the most obvious sites—often those enticing travelers but offering little

Figure 3.5   Herringbone Diagram of the Reforms of the Mexican Constitution of 1917

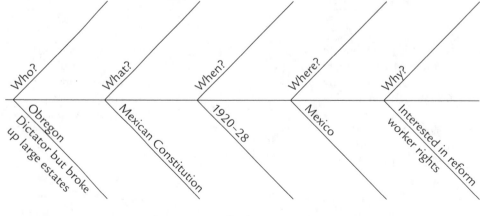

When Textbooks Fall Short

cultural and geographic information. Spelling and typing errors also derailed students' search efforts.

Internet information frequently lacks the traditional structures students are accustomed to in print (lists, comparison/contrast and pro/con dichotomies) and therefore contain too much information with too few road maps for struggling readers. Studies of middle school students' online reading suggests that "young adolescents who are still developing their metacognitive monitoring strategies for comprehension and critical reading can easily experience disorientation online" (McNabb 2006, 22). Indeed, in McNabb's interviews with students about their search strategies, one student said that visually appealing Web pages must be credible, because a great deal of money had been spent designing and supporting the sites.

In connection with an assignment in which small groups had to research a particular figure in the Mexican Revolution and then create a PowerPoint or iMovie presentation, Ty used the following strategy to scaffold and develop his students' independent online reading. Before using it, you may want to conduct a WebQuest or Internet workshop in which you:

- provide direct instruction in searching the Internet
- give students actual URLs (Web addresses) to visit
- model how to make intertextual (cross-site) links
- allow students to share their search findings, frustrations, and successes (Bean et al. 2008; Leu et al. 2004)

Numerous Internet sites (the WebQuest page at San Diego State University, http://webquest.sdsu.edu, for example) offer guidance and examples relative to constructing WebQuests. Additional resources are included in the recommended reading section of this chapter.

Searching Online Resource Texts

Once students are adept at these basic, heavily guided Internet searches, the five-step strategy shown in Figure 3.6, which is based on observations of the metacognitive strategies employed by skilled readers searching websites critically and effectively (McNabb 2006, for example), can be of great help. Each step is important and you can add extra scaffolding initially by restricting the particular sites in a search to a few useful ones. (This series of steps is not a generic prescription applicable to every situation; modify them as necessary.)

Figure 3.6   Searching Online Reading Texts (SORT)

Step 1. Type your topic key word (*Pancho Villa*, for example) into your search engine (Google, for example).

Step 2. Skim (take a brief look) at your search results and eliminate unrelated sites from further consideration.

Step 3. Open the remaining sites and take notes (using your computer's clipboard or similar space).

Step 4. Bookmark each site you visit so you can backtrack if you need to.

Step 5. *Stop* when the information at various sites begins to overlap.

Ty begins independent Internet search activities in his class by encouraging students to read with a critical eye. Not all information and sites yield reliable information; students need to select useful sites and ignore unrelated but often enticing sites (Facebook, for example). Figure 3.7 depicts Shannon Sandoval's search for information on her chosen figure, Pancho Villa, using the searching online resource texts (SORT) strategy.

Ty's Classroom: What We've Learned

Revisit the anticipation-reaction guide from the beginning of the chapter. How have your views changed?

You Can Never Provide Too Much Text Scaffolding and Guidance for Students

When we think about developing students' independent learning with a variety of texts, we generally envision learners who can read, take notes, graphically organize or map concepts, and act on information to produce a paper, project, or multimedia presentation. Indeed, the International Reading Association position statement on adolescent

Figure 3.7 Searching Online Reading Texts (SORT)

Step 1. Type your topic key word (*Pancho Villa*, for example) into your search engine (Google, for example).

Shannon typed in the key word Pancho Villa *on Google, which generated over a million sites.*

Step 2. Skim (take a brief look) at your search results and eliminate unrelated sites from further consideration.

Of the ten sites on page 1, Shannon deleted three. One was seeking information on old friends from school, including a classmate named Pancho Villa. A Facebook site was attempting to contact friends of high school student Pancho Vila (note spelling difference).

Step 3. Open the remaining sites and take notes (using your computer's clipboard or similar space).

The first site Shannon opened featured a photo of Doroteo Arango Arambula, aka Pancho Villa, on his horse. The information included some of what she had read in the class textbook and in Ty's learning packet but included other facts as well. She learned that Pancho Villa appeared as himself in numerous films in the early 1900s. The site also referred to the song "Pancho and Lefty." Additional, less compre-hensive sites contained similar information. Shannon took notes on the information she found.

Step 4. Bookmark each site you visit so you can backtrack if you need to.

Shannon was careful to do this.

Step 5. *Stop* when the information at various sites begins to overlap.

Shannon decided to focus her PowerPoint information on Pancho Villa's media and popular culture notoriety and concluded her search.

literacy highlights this principle as key to competent content-area reading: "Adolescents deserve instruction that builds both the skill and desire to read increasingly complex materials" (Moore et al. 1999, 5). More recently, the *Harvard Educational Review* themed issue devoted to adolescent literacy offered a critical look at cognitive strategy in-struction aimed at developing independent learners in various content areas. Conley (2008) argues that this process is by no means easy. The question is, how do we give students space to develop independent strategy use?

Students Will Read and Study Texts Using the Strategies You Show Them

Ty models picking out essential text information and using the verbatim split page procedure to take notes. Students can also listen to their iPod-recorded notes and rewrite them, thus reencountering key content and concepts, which especially benefits struggling readers (Fisher et al. in press). By having students adopt VSSP for their own independent learning (Conley 2008), Ty helps students like Julia Ruiz and Paul Valerio develop confidence in studying varied texts.

By making connections across diverse texts and multimedia, students are working at an advanced level of content-area literacy that mirrors literacy tasks in the workplace. One of the major difficulties teachers and students confront when using many and varied kinds of texts (traditional textbooks, magazines, Internet blogs and bulletin boards, films, music, and so on) is connecting the concepts found there. The technical term for making connections across text forms is *intertextuality* (Beach 2007). Julia's plan to create an iMovie clip about Pancho Villa is a good example of using intertextual elements (song, film, and text) to capture a major historical figure.

Because Ty uses varied texts and models how to connect ideas found in these sources, his students have a good foundation for creating presentations that mirror this crucial element of advanced reading. Ultimately, Ty releases responsibility to his students so they can experiment independently with strategies like VSSP and use them in their other classes. Clinging to a more heavy-handed approach and guiding students' reading of every text with study questions is likely to result in a kind of learned helplessness on the part of students.

It's Difficult to Learn How to Use Study Strategies Independently

Classroom-based studies suggest the opposite is true, as long as there is careful guidance like Ty gives his students (Fisher et al. in press). Students are generally hungry for ways to cope with the varied kinds of texts they are reading both traditionally and online, and there are any number of study strategies they can use, depending on the content area. No single strategy like VSSP fits all areas (Shanahan and Shanahan 2008).

You can use the example of Ty's teaching and the various strategies he uses in his classroom (VSSP, graphic organizers, Venn diagrams, the herringbone diagram, and SORT) to move students toward powerful independent study. Each of these strategies helps students evaluate varied kinds of texts and begin reading like an insider in the field (Hynd-Shanahan et al. 2005). In this case, Ty piqued his students' interest in history by offering just the right blend of scaffolding and encouraging independence.

Additional Resources on Using the Internet

While the content-area reading and study strategies profiled in this chapter have a strong foundation, using the Internet is still a relatively recent phenomenon. We have provided annotations for the following helpful resources.

Beach, R. 2007. *Teaching Media Literacy.com: A Web-Linked Guide to Resources and Activities*. New York: Teachers College Press.

This is a valuable resource on developing critical media literacy related to WebQuests and other online Internet search activities. The book contains numerous useful websites.

O'Brien, D., and C. Scharber. 2008. "Digital Literacies." *Journal of Adolescent & Adult Literacy* (September). Available at www.reading.org.

This department in the *Journal of Adolescent & Adult Literacy* features ongoing discussions of key issues related to reading online. A blog site is included on which teachers can share and talk about resources.

Leu, D. J., D. D. Leu, and J. Coiro. 2004. *Teaching with the Internet, K–12: New Literacies for New Times*. Norwood, MA: Christopher-Gordon.

This valuable resource features a wealth of research-based strategies that acknowledge the challenges students experience searching the idiosyncratic terrain of the Internet.

McNabb, M. L. 2006. *Literacy Learning in Networked Classrooms: Using the Internet with Middle-Level Students*. Newark, DE: International Reading Association.

The author's extensive and close-grained look at middle-level students' reading online has produced a wealth of guidelines and useful websites for the classroom.

Moorman, G., and J. Horton. 2007. "Millenials and How to Teach Them." In *Adolescent Literacy Instruction: Policies and Promising Practices*, edited by J. Lewis and G. Moorman, 263–85. Newark, DE: International Reading Association.

This article includes lists of useful websites for teachers and students, along with a close look at contemporary adolescent learners.

Open to All

How to Use YouTube and Other Venues to Invite Struggling Readers into the Conversation

4

Madeline teaches high school American literature and junior remedial English classes. She faces the constantly challenging task of how to engage her students, many of whom are struggling readers, in close, interpretive readings of novels that are part of the established literary canon. Madeline embraces multimedia resources and incorporates these powerful learning tools in her teaching. "If I see something I can use, I grab it. I try to bring interesting things into the curriculum in connection with the material we read."

For example, before her students read John Steinbeck's *Of Mice and Men* (1937/2006), Madeline went to the SMART board and accessed the following website on the internet (http://rs6.loc.gov/ammem/afctshtml/tsme.html) so the students could examine the cultural history of the Dust Bowl and workers' migration west. Afterward, she used the accompanying quick-write prompts and questions regarding the social differences profiled in the second chapter of the book. Her struggling readers received a brief, very engaging introduction to the novel.

Web 2.0 (The Second Generation)

In the not very distant past, the Internet (or Web) was largely treated by teachers and students as a repository of information. With the expansion of server storage capacity and broadband access from nearly anywhere on the planet, the Web has taken a giant leap forward to become a giant palette for teacher and student creativity. YouTube, MySpace, Facebook, blogs, and podcast offerings on iTunes and other sites now give teachers and students access to a huge array of multimedia resources. A dizzying collection of video clips, many produced by students as class projects, expand students' visual learning.

Recognizing that global issues are best understood and acted upon by multiple thinkers including students, curriculum development efforts that tap into Web 2.0's interactivity hold tremendous promise. For example, ITGlobal has created a project site where students from around the globe can blog, post art work, and collaborate on global issues like climate change (Tapscott and Williams 2008). In essence, any time you are using multimedia in your teaching, you are getting close to students' worlds outside school (Pahl and Rowsell 2006). Multimedia may include but are not limited to:

- Web pages and Web logs (blogs)
- wikis
- video clips (on YouTube, for example)
- simulations (virtual worlds like Second Life)
- iMovies
- VoiceThread and other podcasts
- songs
- artwork
- texting
- cartoons and comics (ComicLife, for example)
- animated films
- video games
- logos and graphics

The most popular use of the Internet for contemporary teens is the creation of content, particularly student-authored blogs and videos

(Tapscott and Williams 2008). In any recent look at the shifting nature of texts, we see that conventionally printed textbooks are fast being overtaken by the visual world of the screen (Kress 2003). "Reading" these visual media require attention to layout and design elements. The message, to a great extent, is carried by the particular elements that are emphasized. For example, in television advertisements designed to sell a particular product, the brand name and product are prominently displayed.

Reading any type of material involves paying careful attention to how it was constructed (Norman 2004). Since no text is neutral, helping students consider the hidden meanings and power elements is crucial. For example, the widely popular magazine *Cosmopolitan*, available at most grocery store checkout counters, has been around since 1970. It was founded by Helen Gurley-Brown as a sexually liberating counterpoint to women's magazines of the day (van Leeuwen 2005). Today, *Cosmo* spans the globe, portraying women as free-spirited and sexually adventurous but often rendering poorer members of society invisible (van Leeuwen 2005). Any critical reading of this work needs to consider who the audience is, how the design and text elements portray a particular viewpoint, and who is left out of this picture (Stevens and Bean 2007).

Madeline, Phyllis, and Kenneth incorporate second-generation Web resources and other multimedia in their classrooms in much the same way they embraced simulation-type video games and other engaging practices before Web 2.0 came along—not without some anxiety but always focusing on student learning. A willingness to take risks and access to some support mechanisms like colleagues and workshops will help you refine your own approach to using technology and multimedia in the classroom. (We caution that this is a challenging, fast-moving world. You should approach the world of blogs, TeacherTube, YouTube, and other multimedia sites as works-in-progress. Adding multimedia to your lessons and units takes time and careful deliberation. Start small and build from there.)

Classroom Snapshot: Madeline

To get a sense of how these resources enrich concept learning, let's look at a lesson on cloning Madeline introduced in her junior remedial English class, where she frequently brings in supplemental magazine articles and online material as a way to reach struggling readers. She says,

> My junior literacy kids need to develop strategies on how to read for information. In my classroom I use the online edition of *USA Today* [www.usatoday.com], Wikipedia, and video clips from TeacherTube and YouTube. I'm trying to find a way to make reading interesting and help them see there are many different purposes for reading. They have been unable to pass the high school exit exam, so that's also one of the goals. Some of them want to go into a trade, some want to be chefs. I just think that expository texts and online reading material makes sense.

The article and companion multimedia material Madeline found on cloning really engaged these students in a controversial topic.

> The *USA Today* article 'Understanding Cloning' [Holladay 2006] got them started on this topic. Then I directed them to two video clips that shed some more light. I had them use Venn diagrams to compare and contrast various views about ethical dilemmas and cloning, which worked well. We approached the topic of cloning from the standpoint of being able to clone a duplicate of yourself—there is a wonderful student-created spoof of this available on YouTube.

While cloning is generally understood (albeit in a very limited sense), Madeline wanted her students to understand both the scientific reasons for cloning and its ethical ramifications. "Before we read the *USA Today* article, I gave them the opportunity to write about what they knew about cloning on our classroom blog at Blogger.com. Then they shared their ideas with a partner before they read the material and watched and evaluated the video clips."

The two-page *USA Today* article on human cloning described the process of cloning Dolly the sheep and mentioned some of the problems encountered (277 failed attempts, for example). It discussed only the positive features of cloning, including using clones in treating diseases, genetically engineering food crops that are resistant to pests, and mapping genomes.

Given that struggling readers generally need careful scaffolding when they explore the Internet, Madeline guided them to a site where a short video clip introduced information about cloning and revealed that Australia had been given a green light to experiment with human cloning. Unfortunately, like the *USA Today* article, that site failed to deal with any of the ethical issues of human cloning.

The student-produced YouTube video they watched provided a dramatic counterpoint to this very positive view. Entitled *A Human*

Clone!, it featured a high school student advertising a new miracle product called "clonex," a pill you can take to clone yourself. In one scene, the student briefs the clone about all the miserable tasks he wants the clone to do for him during the week, among them "undergoing knee surgery." (The clonex pill also produces every side effect ever mentioned in conventional drug advertisements.) Madeline had pairs of students develop graphic organizers and/or Venn diagrams that displayed the positive and negative aspects of cloning based on the article and videos (see Figure 4.1 for an example).

Then Madeline introduced the SORT strategy (discussed in Chapter 3) for searching the Internet for additional information on cloning ethics. (Many of the strategies introduced in Chapter 3 are applicable to multimedia exposure and critique. The Cornell note-taking strategy, graphic organizers, Venn diagrams, and herringbone diagrams can also be used to help scaffold and organize information gleaned from multimedia sources.) See the student examples below.

Finally, based on everything they had learned, the students, in small groups, created multimedia productions illustrating the positive and negative aspects of human cloning. They could include music (rap, punk rock, blues), short video clips, PowerPoint slides—whatever their

Figure 4.1   Venn Diagram on Cloning Yourself

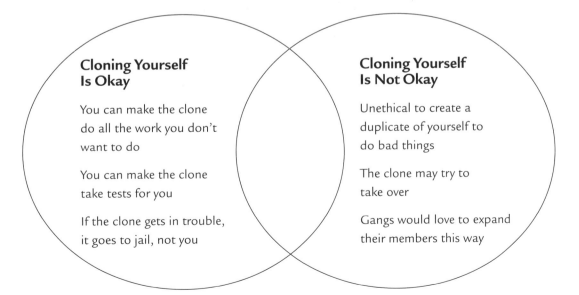

creative imaginations came up with. One student, a drummer, created a drum solo that rose in volume when his group's PowerPoint challenged human cloning on ethical grounds and became less loud at those points where positive features of cloning were being discussed.

Classroom Snapshot: Phyllis

Because Phyllis' eighth-grade language arts class is linked to a colleague's American history class, she is able to introduce her students to authentic readings that go beyond the course literature anthology. An inveterate reader herself, Phyllis frequents used-book stores and has a huge array of many kinds of texts from which she can draw. She is also eager to use multimedia.

Phyllis is dedicated to opening up her students, including struggling and resistant readers, to the power of reading—its potential to expand their world. "I want them to discover how wonderful it is to sit down with a good story or to read a piece of nonfiction and learn something you didn't know before. You open your mind and open your world, expand this place you move around in."

One strategy Phyllis uses is to have students read in pairs.

> I try to pair grade-level kids with struggling readers. I make sure they have time to read to each other, read a little bit at a time and discuss it, paraphrase what they read. We do a lot of 'let's predict' what might happen later in the story. Predict, question, clarify. We use that strategy a lot. We also do readers' theatre. Lately, we've been making short YouTube-style video clips of our readers' theatre productions. The kids enjoy seeing themselves on the screen and SMART Board.

In a unit on the American frontier, Phyllis uses the book *Everyday Life: The Frontier* (Hazen 1999), which tells stories about historical figures in an engaging way and helps students make connections with popular movies about this period. They pick characters to explore in detail, looking at both the reader-friendly descriptions of key figures in the frontier West and adding the in-depth information provided in the required American history textbook.

Then Phyllis has students create skits based on fascinating incidents that took place in frontier towns. She begins by reviewing the characteristics of a good skit:

PHYLLIS: What characterizes a good skit?

STUDENT: Showing a range of emotions.

STUDENT: Using props.

STUDENT: It has to flow.

STUDENT: Creativity.

STUDENT: The actors should be believable.

STUDENT: You need a good audience.

STUDENT: It's worth putting on YouTube!

PHYLLIS: Those are all good points. I want you to write a skit that takes place in a frontier town you select and that illustrates frontier justice, housing problems, or school life. I'll need a written version. On one of the double-period days you can perform it and we'll film it for YouTube.

Phyllis continues the assignment, asking students about the characteristics of dialogue and suggesting they include dialogue (using a western dialect); a foil (or second character) that attempts to prevent the main character from carrying out his or her plan and that the main character outwits; a soliloquy (in which a character talks to him- or herself and the audience learns his or her thoughts and feelings); and staging notes (scene design, music, things that set the mood, etc.).

In Chapter 8 of *Everyday Life: The Frontier*, which deals with vigilante justice, Mark finds the character for his skit—Judge Roy Bean, a larger-than-life Texas character featured in popular Hollywood films as "the hanging judge":

> One of the most famous [vigilante "lawmen"] was Judge Roy Bean of Langtry, Texas. Langtry was a small town populated by workers laying track for the Southern Pacific Railroad. As a typical frontier community, it was rough and disorderly and in dire need of law and order. Roy Bean came on the scene in 1882 and filled that need, even though in sometimes comic fashion. (60)

Mark's creativity begins perking as he envisions himself as a comedic criminal named *Mr.* Bean (Mark is a fan of the character by this name created by British slapstick comic Rowan Atkinson), a natural foil for *Judge* Roy Bean, played by his friend Randy. He reads on:

> Bean was a drifter of questionable character who managed to get himself appointed justice of the peace in Langtry. He set up court in a shack that doubled as a courtroom and saloon. Ever looking to fill his pockets with a dollar, Judge Bean once fined a dead man $40 for illegally carrying a weapon. The dead man, of course, had exactly that amount on his person. (61)

That nails it. Mark can already see the ending for his short skit: Randy, as Judge Roy Bean, fining a dead Mr. Bean, as played by himself. He'll borrow his baby brother's small electric car as a stand-in for Mr. Bean's ever-present yellow Mini Cooper.

He watches some YouTube video clips on Mr. Bean and Judge Roy Bean to prepare for writing his own somewhat twisted look at frontier justice—clips from the movie about Judge Roy Bean starring Paul Newman, as well as a collection of Mr. Bean clips, including one of Mr. Bean acting silly in front of a jail two-way mirror. Then Mark and his friend Randy create a skit based on Judge Roy Bean's encounter with Bad Bob, an outlaw who rode into Langtry to terrorize the people. Mr. Bean (Mark, wearing Atkinson's characteristic tweed coat and tie and uttering not a line of dialogue) replaces Bad Bob. As Mr. Bean, Mark points his fingers ("six guns") at Roy Bean's saloon, calling for him to come out and fight. The skit ends with Mr. Bean's demise on the streets of Langtry, Texas, after Judge Roy Bean shot him in the back with a paint gun as Mr. Bean calls one last time for the judge to come out and fight fair and square. The comic quality of their spoof earns Mark and Randy an A, and the video is archived as a model for other students in future classes.

A group of girls in Phyllis' class use their skit to demonstrate the frontier's harsh living conditions—families huddled through the winter in sod houses on the prairies. These students research the harsh conditions of women's life on the prairie (while the sod homes were sturdy and warm, they often leaked in severe rainstorms, they were damp, and they allowed rodents and other pests in) and then, in their skit, juxtapose the sparse furnishings and minimalist dirt brick structures of frontier life with today's technology (cell phones, for example). Phyllis says:

> I was trying to show them that frontier women are sometimes going to be larger-than-life characters. Maybe they drove the wagon themselves or built the house because their husbands were our herding cattle or were killed on the way out West. So you see ordinary people doing extraordinary things.

Phyllis engages students in discussions about the accuracy and authenticity of information in their readings about the frontier. She continually encourages her students to verify facts using many and varied texts, since some of the larger-than-life characters may have been figments of dime novel writers' imaginations as they spun a particularly dramatic picture of cowboys and frontier law. Contemporary

When Textbooks Fall Short

westerns like *Appaloosa* do little to tarnish this overly heroic image, but more down-to-earth accounts of gun fights and frontier justice suggest that the classical gunfight was largely a myth. Outlaws and good guys were just as likely to get shot in the back—as in Mark and Randy's skit.

Melding the Old and the New

In our teaching, how can we integrate the old print-based elements with the more fluid and captivating visual features of the Internet? Blogs, podcasts, and even the more familiar PowerPoint productions students develop have a wide array of support in much of the contemporary work on new literacies. As you attempt to tap the power of new technology, remember you are not alone in figuring out how to blend the old and new. A number of educators are producing useful resources you can consult as you plan creative lessons and units in your classroom. We highlight a few of these resources below and include an annotated list at the end of the chapter.

Knobel and Lankshear's *A New Literacies Sampler* (2007) features edited chapters on a host of topics that address critical issues as you endeavor to expand your use of multimodal resources in the classroom. Stone (2007) provides a framework for critically evaluating website content. Similarly, Callow (2008) has developed a system for assessing students' visual literacy that takes into account many of the properties important in a screen-dominated project (layout choices, use of color, images, etc.).

Students in content-area classes like Phyllis' and Madeline's are creating their preferred identities, often online. For example, West (2008) charts her students' literary blog identities in eleventh-grade American literature. Her students assumed a range of literate identities, from serious critic of literary works to pop-cultural humorist. West notes: "When I announced upcoming blogging sessions to my class, their excitement was palpable. In their minds, blogging was fun, and a sense of play permeated the most successful (and popular) blog entries" (597).

As a means of scaffolding blogging in your class, you may want to use a process our graduate students call "tabletop blogging." Give students a large piece of colored poster paper with an image they can react to in the middle of the page (in a unit on immigration, for example, you might use a photo of an immigration policy protest parade). Students then write down their comments, as the poster circulates from one student (or small group of students) to another. This simulates participating in an online blog and points up the necessity of code-shifting from street language (e.g., profanity) to more sophisticated discourse when responding online. (A ground rule like this doesn't mean students shouldn't use invented spellings and other informal features typical of blogging and text messaging.)

When your students are tackling more elaborate projects involving digital movie composition or developing YouTube-like spoofs on advertisements, other resources may be helpful. For example, Renee Hobbs' *Reading in the Media* (2007) features a system for helping students analyze advertisements. In addition, Hobbs offers other critical media literacy questions designed to help students see media productions as creations open to critique.

Making digital movies is very popular among adolescents. The cloning example and spoof mentioned earlier in the chapter hints at the potential of this medium for learning content. Our favorite YouTube productions are those students create in response to topics they have studied in their content-area classes.

High school economics teachers can use an ever-growing array of resources, including the virtual trading of currencies in multiplayer online games (called MMOGS) like *EverQuest* or *Second Life* (http://secondlife.com/) (Steinkuehler 2008).

Video games like SimCity are yet another way to immerse students in economic principles like supply and demand. Squire (2008) notes that "gamers have grown up in simulated worlds, worlds where anything is possible, and where learning through trial and error is expected" (654).

Classroom Snapshot: Kenneth

Gaming has been an integral part of Kenneth's repertoire of techniques for teaching economics for some time. It is yet another way to help students explore sometimes slippery discourse and concepts. Much as Phyllis uses print and multimedia resources to immerse students in hands-on video productions, Kenneth uses traditional and virtual simulations to help students comprehend the arcane concepts associated with economic theory and practice. "I try to give them a number of ways to acquire the concepts. I get them involved in simulations and group work, have them talk to each other, because I am not the fountain of all wisdom." Kenneth's philosophy of teaching economics is grounded in the notion that "economics is the study of choices by individuals, economies, governments, business communities, etc. Whenever a choice is made it leads to an opportunity cost or a trade-off. I want the kids to be aware in the beginning that economics is not exclusively about the study of money."

The availability of Web 2.0 tools to foster student creativity opens a floodgate of possibilities. YouTube offers a vast collection of product video clips (the simulation example here taps into two of them). In addition, Kenneth favors visual learning tools like graphic organizers, herringbone diagrams, and Venn diagrams to get students to compare and contrast issues and concepts.

Kenneth challenges his students to understand that the seemingly simple idea of supply and demand is anything but simple: "We talk about shifts in supply and demand, looking closely at their elasticity. I want students to understand how much supply and demand are driven by price change."

In this simulation, aimed at making the potentially abstract law of demand transparent, Kenneth places students in two groups. One group is affiliated with a new bicycle company successfully manufacturing energy-efficient, battery-augmented bicycles that will allow their owners to commute up to twenty miles to work, even over challenging hills. This bike company, called XTrac, is attracting an enthusiastic audience of consumers but is still a small company using Thailand-based labor to manufacture the bike frames and small battery packs. While demand for this product is escalating, the supply of bikes XTrac is able to offer for sale is sporadic at best.

In contrast, DinoBike has been making non-battery-supported, heavy-frame bikes for years. They are durable, resemble classic beach cruisers, and nearly useless for commuting to work in a gas crisis. While DinoBike has plenty of inventory, their supply exceeds the demand. In a U.S. market economy, DinoBike is likely to fail. However, the government is thinking about stepping in to subsidize DinoBike in its efforts to retool and begin to build lightweight bikes with battery support in order to compete with the foreign upstart XTrac.

In this simulation students review the video clips highlighting their respective bicycles and then argue their company needs, based on their awareness of the principles of self-interest and supply and demand. The overarching questions Kenneth poses for them are:

- What is the best course of action for your company?
- How do the economic principles of supply and demand and cost figure in your argument?

As a prelude to carrying out this simulation, Kenneth's students read the textbook section headed "Supply and the Law of Demand." Kenneth tells them they can use herringbone diagrams to develop their arguments, as well as any media that might help illustrate the value of their argument.

Both the XTrac and DinoBike groups meet to discuss their strategies and develop arguments addressing the two questions. They then debate the relative merits of each company and propose courses of action (charted in herringbone diagrams—see Figures 4.2 and 4.3).

Let's listen in:

KENNETH: Okay, let's start with DinoBike, the older company, and your plans to rebuild this aging firm.

DINO S1: We're a classic bike and lots of people love our beach cruisers. We just need to advertise better.

Figure 4.2 Herringbone Diagram for Supply and Demand—XTrac

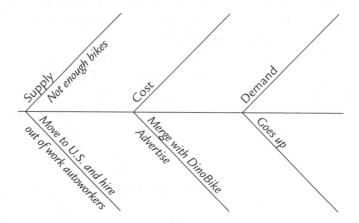

Figure 4.3   Herringbone Diagram for Supply and Demand—DinoBike

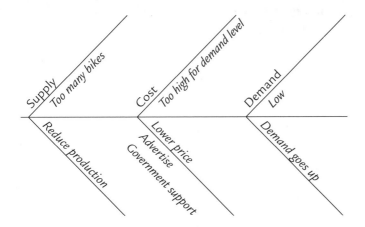

DINO S2: I found a great YouTube video that shows an electric bike out of control and crashing. They are too fast for some people.

KENNETH: Okay, but how are you going to address the fundamental economic problem—DinoBike has too much inventory, so their supply outpaces demand for this product.

DINO S3: We could do what the oil companies do, at least OPEC, and reduce our production.

DINO S4: Yeah, that would help in the long run, but I think we need to lower the price of our bikes and sell out our current inventory. Then DinoBikes will be rare and that will buy us some time to retool, maybe adding electric bikes to our line.

DINO S1: Then we could produce a new advertisement about our new line but let people know that they are in good hands with this well-established company, not some foreign upstart. Take a look at the Marrs Cycle ad on YouTube. It looks like a pretty cool electric beach cruiser.

DINO S3: We could ask for a government bailout like the car companies. That would buy us some time, and we could then construct prototypes for our own electric bike or buy out the Marrs Company if it's pretty small.

KENNETH: Great ideas. Let's also hear from the XTrac group. How are you going to solve the problem of not enough inventory and high demand for your electric bikes manufactured too slowly in Thailand?

XTRAC S1: I think we need to move our manufacturing plant back to the United States and hire unemployed auto workers to assemble our product at home.

XTRAC S2: What about merging with DinoBike to form one company that could build both new light electric bikes and the classic cruiser models?

XTRAC S3: The videos on YouTube about electric bikes show how powerful they can be for commuting to work, even on challenging hills. Take a look at "Mike's View on Electric Bikes" where he talks about riding home from work on his slick $3000 bike and getting passed on a hill by an older lady on an electric bike!

XTRAC S4: Yeah, take a look at the "Electric Bike Commercial" [http://www.youtube.com/watch?v=8ug7mzr8zrA8Y].

KENNETH: Okay, a lot of good ideas. Each group needs to develop a business plan that links these ideas to key economic concepts about supply and demand. You can certainly include creative YouTube ads that you and your group create to advertise your respective bike companies.

Kenneth's students also learn how to draw a "demand curve," which encompasses the classical law that when prices drop, demand increases. Kenneth notes, "I try to model my tests after the state examination, which follows the state standards. Then, when my kids take the state exam they are going to do better. My students have the highest pass rates in the school."

Combining various types of texts, including an economics textbook, primary sources, newspaper articles, CNN news clips on government bailouts, YouTube video clips, and other media resources, Kenneth helps his students to grasp the key terminology of his discipline in ways they can apply. By centering this activity on manufacturing electric bikes, he develops student interest and has them review multimedia sources readily available on the Internet.

What We've Learned

Madeline, Phyllis, and Kenneth each take creative risks to engage students' interest in multimodal learning. By integrating print-based metacognitive strategies like Venn diagrams and herringbone diagrams with newer media available on the Internet (YouTube, for example), they tap into students' creative talents. Many other teachers we have had the good fortune to work with and study in our classroom research take these kinds of risks. We recommend you give some of these practices a try, particularly those that ask learners to be active, creative developers of multimedia within the unique demands of English, social studies, economics, and other content areas.

Additional Resources to Try

Print Based

Callow, J. 2008. "Show Me: Principles for Assessing Students' Visual Literacy." *The Reading Teacher* 61 (8): 616–26.

Callow has created a system for assessing students' visual literacy that is also useful as a teaching aid in instructing students about aspects of visual design.

Coiro, J., M. Knobel, C. Lankshear, and D. J. Leu. 2008. *Handbook of Research on New Literacies*. Mahwah, NJ: Lawrence Erlbaum.

This is a landmark work encompassing all the major subtopics of digital literacies (or new literacies), including video gaming. The authors are key players in this fast-moving field.

Hobbs, R. 2007. *Reading the Media: Media Literacy in High School English*. New York: Teachers College Press.

The author takes a detailed look at helping students critically evaluate advertisements and think about the aesthetics of visual design.

O'Brien, D., and C. Scharber. 2008. "Digital Literacies Go to School: Potholes and Possibilities." *Journal of Adolescent & Adult Literacy* 52 (1): 66–68.

This JAAL department discusses issues related to new literacies and regularly features recommended websites.

Moje, E. B. 2008. "Foregrounding the Disciplines in Secondary Literacy Teaching and Learning: A Call for Change." *Journal of Adolescent & Adult Literacy* 52 (2): 96–107.

This article has a related podcast at the JAAL homepage (click on the issue).

Pahl, K., and J. Rowsell. 2005. *Literacy and Education: Understanding the New Literacy Studies in the Classroom.* London: Paul Chapman.

This highly readable introduction to new literacies features many classroom examples.

Stone, J. C. 2007. "Popular Websites in Adolescents' Out-of-School Lives: Critical Lessons on Literacy." In *A New Literacies Sampler,* edited by M. Knobel and C. Lankshear, 49–63. New York: Peter Lang.

This chapter focuses on a framework students can use to analyze popular websites like *Seventeen* and *ArcadePod*.

West, K. C. 2008. "Weblogs and Literacy Response: Socially Situated Identities and Hybrid Social Languages in English Class Blogs." *Journal of Adolescent & Adult Literacy* 51 (7): 588–98.

This author provides a good introduction to blogging in English classes with examples that illustrate the value of using blogging in your classroom.

Media Based

In addition to TeacherTube, YouTube, Filamentality, and numerous other online resources, interactive wikis let teachers read, view, and listen to podcasts, blogs, and other forums related to lesson and unit planning and discussion, as well as participate in "teacher affinity" chat rooms and message boards. Here are a three websites to get you started:

- www.blog.reading.org/jaal: sponsored by the *Journal of Adolescent & Adult Literacy*
- www.reading.org: the International Reading Association features an array of podcasts
- www.newlits.org: an excellent website with an array of online authors and resources, as well as a wiki feature that lets you participate in discussions and add information about using new literacies in your teaching

Curl Up with a Good Book 2.0

Book Talks, Discussion Threads, and Other Strategies for Teaching Critical Reading Online

E very ninth-grade English teacher knows that capturing student interest can be as challenging as separating teenagers from their cell phones. Brenda knows it better than most. She teaches in an online public high school with students she rarely sees. Some of them are in juvenile facilities, and most have long, sad histories in traditional educational settings they've since departed, by choice or request. Each fall, Brenda sends her students an email asking how she can make online learning work for them. Sandra's response is typical:

> I daydream way too much and when I start doing that I stop paying attention and when it comes to having to do the work I don't know anything because I started daydreaming! So it has to be fun!!

Brenda thinks she knows what Sandra means by *fun*: something relevant to her life. Every day Brenda scours the real and virtual worlds for material that will connect with her students. The things she does, like introducing a novel with a "book talk" she's filmed using digital storytelling software, may seem far removed from activities in a traditional classroom. But really, she's serving the goals shared by every teacher, using technological tools and resources that enable students to develop critical literacy practices—to move beyond passively accepting everything that is written in texts, whether those texts may be Internet posts, novels, newspapers, music lyrics, ads, films, video games, or comic strips. Because critical literacy views readers as active participants, it is a powerful way for students to become aware of how texts are positioned in certain ways.

About the School

Brenda teaches at a distance education charter school with a diverse student population. The demographics for 2007–2008 were 20 percent Hispanic, 12 percent African American, and 60.9 percent white, and the percentages of Hispanic and African American students are increasing. The percentage of students with special needs is also increasing. Currently, more than 15 percent of the students have an individualized educational plan (IEP). The annual yearly progress (AYP) rating for the last four years has been "needs to improve."

As a distance education charter school, Brenda's school strives to implement new and innovative ways to help the students succeed. Students are required to attend school in person one day a week, from 8 A.M.–12 noon or 12 noon–4 P.M. During this four-hour block, students spend one hour in homeroom, one hour in math lab, and two hours in a project-based course centered on developing social skills. Her school also has a learning lab, which is open five days a week, 8 A.M. to 4 P.M., to all students, especially those who have Internet problems or no working computer at home. Each certified teacher spends two hours a week tutoring or mentoring students in the learning lab.

The school is open, at no cost, to any student residing in the county. Its mission revolves around four core values: commitment, respect, flexibility, and optimism. It believes that all students are unique and that by using sound instructional practices and providing varied avenues for students to demonstrate comprehension, they can achieve academic success.

Challenges of Online Teaching

Teaching high school students online is challenging, especially when the students believe the public school system has failed them. In Brenda's class, some students have been homeschooled all their lives;

When Textbooks Fall Short

others have fled traditional public schools because of peer pressure. Some have flunked out, been expelled, or been placed in a juvenile facility. How does teaching them online work?

First, it is imperative to get to know them as soon as possible. To do so, she relies heavily on technology tools and resources. Each fall, she creates a short video using a Webcam and TeacherTube (www .teachertube.com) to introduce herself to the students. Students can see and hear Brenda share her hobbies and encourage them to contact her by phone, email, or face-to-face if they have any questions or concerns. In this learning environment, it is so easy for students to develop a closer bond with their computer than with Brenda and their peers (Zucker and Kozma 2003). To lessen the chances that this will happen, she attends every homeroom within the first two weeks of school to introduce herself. Because most of her ninth graders are new to distance education learning, it is important to make them feel comfortable. If they don't, it is very difficult for them to succeed academically. So Brenda makes it a point to be visible and available.

Understanding the different ways students learn is especially important in this environment. In the past, Brenda has designed critical literacy activities without consulting her students. Brenda assumed that because it was an online class, her students would automatically be enthusiastic and eager to engage in critical literacy practices. She didn't consider different learning styles. Most assignments required them to write essays or short responses. She found herself constantly explaining how to complete the assignments, and even then, most of her students didn't do so. Brenda decided the problem was online education. As a former traditional public school teacher, she began to think online education was not the best route for these students.

At one point, Brenda considered returning to the traditional classroom, and a colleague suggested she think about the following:

- learning styles
- learners' desired outcome
- prior learning experiences.

She gave Brenda a copy of Pamela Dupin-Bryant and Barbara DuCharme-Hansen's "Assessing Student Needs in Web-Based Distance Education" (2005). After reading what researchers in the field had to say about teaching online, Brenda realized that she needed to give her students opportunities to express their concerns about the class.

So, each fall Brenda asks her students to complete a learning styles questionnaire online (http://usd.edu/~bwjames/tut/learning). After students complete the questionnaire, they are directed to a detailed summary about their learning style: visual, auditory, or kinesthetic.

As part of the assignment, Brenda asked students to submit three or four complete sentences summarizing their learning style. They did this using Google Docs (www.docs.google.com), a free Web-based word processing, spreadsheet, and presentation program that lets students and teachers create, store, share, and edit documents online while collaborating in real time with others in the class. The administration requires all teachers to use Google Docs because students don't need to download software, all work is stored safely online, students can access files anytime from any computer, and teachers are able to offer comments and suggestions at any point in the assignment.

Here's Todd's feedback:

> Mostly I am a visual learner because I can easily learn from charts, graphs, books, anything that I can see. I can also learn from listening to things. These are the ways that I learn about things the easiest. Since I am a visual learner obviously I would learn from watching stuff, reading, observing, and looking over the material a couple of times. Since I can also learn from listening to stuff, I need to listen to material provided a couple of times.

Todd needs multimedia tools and resources, including video and audio clips, to help him engage in assigned material. Amber, on the other hand, is a kinesthetic learner:

> After taking the learning style survey I learned that I am a kinesthetic learner. Usually it is somewhat complicated for me to understand something without someone showing or teaching me about the subject. I get distracted easily. That is one reason why this school will be more difficult and challenging for me. Since I have always gone to a regular public school, it is hard for me to understand certain subjects over a computer screen. If I talk to you about some assignments personally, I should be able to stay on track.

Like Sandra, Amber gets distracted easily. She needs hands-on experiences and opportunities to interact with others.

Sandra, Todd, and Amber are not looking forward to completing computer-graded quizzes and tests. They, along with all the other students, are expecting to participate in a learning environment that is fun yet relies heavily on multimedia resources and tools to give them the instruction and scaffolding they need to challenge them and help them succeed academically. While adhering to state standards, Brenda makes it a point to engage students with multimedia resources, including audio and video clips and other technology tools, to help them as they set out on a yearlong journey to develop and verbalize their ideas, improve their competence, seek out multiple perspectives, adopt critical stances, and produce their own alternative text (Beach and O'Brien 2008).

A Digital Book Talk on
Edward Bloor's Novel *Crusader*

In order to accomplish these goals, Brenda had to locate interesting material. Because most students play video games, she uses the award-winning novel *Crusader*, by young adult author Edward Bloor, as the core text for her unit on the novel. It takes approximately nine weeks to complete the unit, and she gives students who get a late start or read more slowly than their classmates extra time to finish.

Because of its graphic content, *Crusader* is seldom taught in traditional public school classrooms. In this learning environment, however, it's easier for her to do so. Although it is very long, with subplots having to do with racism, teenage suicide, lying politicians, abandonment, and violence, it enables students to draw on their cultural knowledge to analyze, in particular, how video games have hidden messages and can stir up ethnic hatred in the people who play them. Most students have never had the opportunity to analyze the messages conveyed in video games.

Brenda introduces the novel to parents and students through a short digital book talk—a visual explanation of why they should read the book. Using Microsoft Photo Story 3.0 (http://www.microsoft.com/windowsxp/using/digitalphotography/photostory/default.mspx)—a free software download from Windows via TeacherTube (www.teachertube.com)—she focuses on the idea of negative messages in video games.

She begins with a rhetorical question: can a video game lead someone to commit a crime? Over jazz music playing softly in the background, Brenda mentions the 2005 Alabama court case in which Devon Moore's attorney argued that childhood abuse and the video game *Grand Theft Auto* caused Moore to murder three police officers (http://www.cbsnews.com/stories/2005/07/13/earlyshow/living/parenting/main708794.shtml).

She then discusses how Roberta, the *Crusader* protagonist, notices the distorted views of those who play the video game and decides to quit the arcade and find the person who murdered her mother:

> This novel centers on fifteen-year-old Roberta, whose mother is murdered while working at the family-owned virtual-reality arcade in a suburban shopping mall. Roberta, feeling lonely and helpless, goes to live with her previously estranged father. She, too, works in the arcade, and dreads going there. One day a new, extremely racist video war game called *Crusader* is delivered. The game portrays Arab people as evil. Patrons rush to play the video game, and Roberta begins to notice the distorted views that the arcade's clientele have. She notices the xenophobia of people who engage in virtual violence. Sam, a nineteen-year-old Arab American who owns Crescent Electronics, a business in the same mall, is harassed because of his ethnicity and religion. He believes the game, and by extension the arcade and Roberta, is responsible. Finally, Roberta breaks from her family and stands up for what she believes; in some ways, Roberta becomes her own crusader as she searches for the person who murdered her mother.

Brenda goes on to explain why she's chosen the novel for her students to read, and ask students and their parents to use it as a springboard to talk with their family and friends about ways to dispel ethnic hatred and promote social equality. Winding up, she highlights some key themes: perseverance, racism, abandonment, and honesty. Brenda concludes by suggesting that both parents and students read the comments on this book that students have posted at www.commonsensemedia.com.

Alternative Novels

Students who find *Crusader* too graphic or too difficult can choose from these alternatives:

- *Tasting the Sky*, by Ibtisam Barakat. A memoir about growing up as a Palestinian in the war-torn West Bank in the 1980s.
- *Esperanza Rising*, by Pam Munoz Ryan. A novel about a young girl who has grown up in an extremely wealthy family; then a tragedy strikes and her family faces difficult economic obstacles.
- *Tears of a Tiger*, by Sharon Draper. A novel about a young man whose self-esteem is shattered after he kills his best friend in a car accident. He faces many challenges before he decides to commit suicide.

While these novels do not deal with all the issues in Bloor's novel, they address at least one of its major themes, which are racism, perseverance, social injustice, pride, and politics. Providing a number of texts with similar themes gives students the opportunity to critique the values and voices that are being promoted.

In an online learning environment, it is important to offer options, especially ones students can download and have read to them by voice recognition software. (Our students can get copies of voice software from our technology department to download on their home computer. Brenda prefers Cepstral because the recordings are less robotic.)

In addition, the school library has copies of books for students who cannot afford to purchase them or aren't able to go to a local library. Most books in the library are either purchased by the school or donated by students. Brenda asks students to sign a checkout sheet to ensure they return the book. And she offers extra credit to students who donate their copy to the school's library. (Christopher, a student, purchased two extra copies of *Crusader* and gave them to Brenda at the end of the year. He said he wanted to make sure that at least two other students had the opportunity to read it!)

Online Discussion Threads

After watching the book talk, students have an opportunity to express their thoughts and respond to their peers' comments in a threaded online discussion. According to Cathie English (2007), a threaded online discussion offers advantages that "real-time" literature discussions in classrooms do not (56). One is that it allows the teacher and students to expand the classroom beyond the school walls so that more thoughtful exchanges can take place. Another is that it provides space for all students to express themselves.

For this assignment, Brenda asks students to respond to a statement made by Devon Moore, the convicted murderer who claimed the *Grand Theft Auto* video game caused him to kill three police officers ("Life is like a video game. Everybody got to die sometime") and to a cartoon (http://www.toothpastefordinner.com/022305/video-games -influence-kids.gif) that reads:

> i don't think video games influence kids . . . i mean, if they did, there'd be an entire internet subculture based around them, and people would stay up late every night playing them, waking up in the afternoon and pausing only to post on the internet about video games.

Brenda also asks them to tell her, in three or four sentences, about a video game that they would create if given the chance. For extra credit, they can also respond to their peers' posts.

Mariah wrote:

> In the case of Grand Theft Auto, play the game and it'll have you breaking into cars and driving them recklessly to who knows where, which is really bad because there are people of all ages, whether it is child, teen, or adult, that play these games and think, like the convicted murderer, that it is okay to do this in the real world. But then on the other side there are games out there like the Leap Frog learning games that actually induct the necessary subjects like math, English, and reading into the games, so that the children playing it will still be having fun but at the same time they're also being taught that learning can be fun. If I could create a game I would probably keep the violence, crude language, and inappropriate/suggestive content at a minimum. And in this game I'd create three scenarios, each with a separate playing field for girls and guys: one for the younger children, another for teenagers and young adults, and the last for the actual adults. I would try to convey messages that would be productive in the process of increasing one's intellectual abilities in ways that will capture the interest and challenge the mind.

Mariah, who is extremely shy, enrolled in the school because she has anxiety attacks. When Mariah first enrolled, the school's counselor asked if Brenda would reassure Mariah that she would meet friendly people at the school. Brenda promised Mariah that she would, so she finally decided to attend homeroom. Periodically, she had an anxiety attack and had to leave the classroom. Although she struggles, Mariah's comment on the discussion thread is thought provoking. In response to Mariah, Steve wrote:

> I disagree with Mariah. I do believe the messages in video games are ruining our society and the people. I don't believe it makes us kill— that is out of the question for me—but I do believe that it's making America fat and causing us to lose sight to live our lives. We ignore priorities, responsibilities, and goals. You don't become successful as a person or in life by sitting down all day and staring at the screen. The messages video games send people are blind to you, but I do believe it has one priority and that's to distract you. Look at the greatest people in the world there are. None of them played video games every day. I'm pretty sure all the way from artists, musicians, athletes, million dollar businessmen, writers, etc.

Threaded online discussions are a safe way for Brenda's students to voice their thoughts and opinions and present a number of perspectives. It empowers students like Mariah to share their thoughts without fearing harsh criticism.

An Effective Online Reading Strategy

Brenda uses the K-W-L (already know, want to know, learned) reading strategy to help students avoid distractions as they consult a number of websites to get background information. Bloor did not include the Crusades video game in the book for entertainment purposes: it's there to convey a message. In the game, Arabs are portrayed as evil; in order to win, patrons have to kill them. Sam Ramad, who owns a business in the West End Mall, is mistreated by some people just because he is an Arab American who happens to be Muslim. Because most students won't understand Sam's hostility and paranoia, she uses the K-W-L reading strategy to guide them as they read excerpts from Bernard Lewis's (1990) article "The Roots of Muslim Rage" in *The Atlantic* magazine (http://www.theatlantic.com/doc/199009/muslim-rage). (On his website, Edward Bloor suggests that students read this article to understand a Muslim perspective on the Crusades.) This assignment allows students to read about people whose voices typically aren't heard; they can explore why certain perspectives are normally privileged, while others are silenced. Because Lewis' article may be difficult for some students to read, Brenda uses excerpts and also provides a link to a Wikipedia site (http://en.wikipedia.org/wiki/Crusades) that includes background information on the historical context of the Crusades. She gives students the following questions:

- What do you *know* about the Crusades? Have you ever heard anything about Crusades? Where and when did you read something about the Crusades?
- What do you *want to know* about the Crusades?
- After reading the background information, what did you *learn* about the Crusades?

Brenda also has students answer these same questions about Edward Bloor in relation to the material on these two websites:

- http://biography.jrank.org/pages/983/Bloor-Edward-William -1950.html.
- URL:http://www.bookbrowse.com/author_interviews/full/index .cfm?author_number=1388.

Exposing her students to this kind of background information enables them to understand why characters respond the way they do to social injustice. This novel really captures the xenophobia, racial tension, drug addiction, violence, and other pressures that some teenagers face in life.

Final Project

Teaching online requires giving students several avenues to express their thoughts, display creativity, and demonstrate comprehension. For the final project, however, most students chose to write a response to one of the writing prompts listed below.

CHARACTER ANALYSIS CHART AND WRITING TO A PROMPT

The first option is to complete a character analysis chart (http://www2.scholastic.com/content/collateral_resources/pdf/u/unit_characteranalysis_characteranalysis.pdf) for one character in the novel. (Because this novel is more than three hundred pages long, Brenda gives them the character analysis chart to help them stay focused. More important, it helps them identify and critique gaps that exist in the character's viewpoints; make connections, if possible; and provide an alternative perspective that challenges the character's point of view.) After completing the chart students then respond to one of the writing prompts below. Students who have chosen to read other novels are given similar book-based writing prompts.

- In rage, Mr. Archer stated, "You really want to know why I can't control my students? I'll tell you. After they leave this school, and for the rest of their lives, the whites stick with the whites, the blacks stick with the blacks, the Spanish stick with the Spanish, and so on. That's what people do. They stick with their own kind. You people don't know a thing about education. You have no idea what's going on in public schools. You expect us to mix all these kids together and to have them live in peace and love and harmony. Well, that's a crock! It's never been that way, and it's never going to be that way. These people don't like each other. They don't like each other when they're teenagers, and they don't like each other when they're adults, either. That's just the way it is. There's your answer. Now leave me alone" (284–85). If you had the opportunity to respond to Mr. Archer's claim, would you agree or disagree? Explain in four or five paragraphs the reasons you may agree or disagree with Mr. Archer. Make sure you use examples to support your claim.

- The title of this novel is *Crusader*. This word *crusade* has several definitions. One is "a vigorous concerted movement for a cause or against an abuse." Identify a character in the novel who sought to stop some form of injustice or abuse. Use examples from the novel to support your claim. In your conclusion, discuss whether or not you would have handled the situation the way the character did and explain why.

- Before Mr. Herman quit teaching, he lectured to the class. He stated, "I have talked to you in the past about careers, and about standards. I have tried to show you how high standards developed in the career of journalism, and about how these standards have slowly been eroding. Let me talk to you today about life itself, and about something higher than the highest standards. About ideals. Plato said that the highest expression of anything—love, truth, friendship—lies in its ideal. But here's the problem: That ideal does not exist here, in reality. It does not exist in our grimy little world. It exists high above it; it can never be reached. It is the standard against which all love, truth, friendship, and so on are to be measured. . . . Now you, as a young person, may have no faith in your country, or in your church, or in your family. But you can still have faith in an ideal. If you have an ideal in front of you, you will never get lost on the journey of life. It is, after all, the journey that matters. So I wish all of you a safe one. Good-bye" (283–48). In four or five paragraphs, explain what Mr. Herman was talking about. What message is he trying to convey or tell the class? Use examples to explain what he meant in his lecture.

Here is Taylor's response to the second prompt:

> *Crusade*; the definition of this word is "a vigorous concerted movement for a cause or against an abuse." Now in *Crusader* there was a lot of racism but one character in the book stood out to me that was really trying hard to fight against it, that was Samir Ramad.
>
> Samir, or Sam, was a Muslim that owned Crescent Electronics in the West End Mall. I think he was probably the only minority in the mall, and some people treated him very wrong. There was even an arcade game where your objective was to kill Arabs. So Sam was not really getting the right treatment, but nothing ever too big happened to him, until one time.

One day when Sam left the mall he walked out to his car and the Star of David was painted on his car, which is a Jewish sign that is completely offensive to a Muslim. The attacks of racism followed as his star got painted too, and his car got keyed. Sam now hired a detective to go to the Arcade and to investigate; there he found a suspect, Hugh James. So Sam pursued Hugh and got him arrested, but when Hugh was under house arrest, he ran out in the middle of the street and got himself run over by a car and killed. But, before that, Sam and Roberta caught someone else while they were spying in one of the shops by Crescent Electronics, Colonel Ritter.

Sam had felt extremely bad when he found out that Hugh died, and paid for his grave and got him shipped to Georgia to be buried. But Sam pursued Colonel Ritter, but eventually dropped the charges. So I don't think Sam ever had a problem again.

If it were me, I probably would have done the same exact thing, but probably not, out of the goodness of my heart drop the charges against Colonel Ritter. But after reading this I have really realized how bad racism is and feel bad about some of my actions, and I hope that people stop worrying about the color on the outside, and start looking on the inside.

Applying Critical Literacy to a Short Story

Teaching novels to high school students in an online environment can be very challenging, which is why Brenda also teaches short stories. The term *short* really means a lot to her students. Brenda finds most students submit assignments that do not require a lot of time to complete. She also finds that most students really enjoy reading fiction set in the future. In this particular case, Brenda's students enjoy reading the short story "Harrison Bergeron" by Kurt Vonnegut, Jr. In the short story, the individual overseeing all handicaps imposed on individuals to ensure equality is the United States Handicap General, Diana Moon Glampers. Before reading the short story, Brenda asks her students to write a 200–250 word paragraph explaining what equality means to them and if it really exists in our society. She believes allowing students to write about equality first enables them to engage in critical literacy practices by deconstructing the way it is presented in the story.

It also makes students use their own understandings to determine who really has power in a futuristic society that presents itself as equal. After completing the first assignment, students then go to the following website to read the story:

http://instruct.westvalley.edu/lafave/hb.html

DESIGNING A CARTOON STRIP

While reading the story, Brenda advises her students to think about the questions listed below:

1. Where did this story take place?

2. When did this story take place?

3. How does the setting capture equality? Who seems to be in control? What type of leader is the Handicap General? What does her title "Handicap General" tell you about her? Why do you think the author made the Handicap General a female and not male? What is he saying or not saying about women in charge?

4. In what ways could the author change the story but still capture the overall message on equality?

5. If you could write your own "Harrison Bergeron" story, how would you capture equality, what would equality look like in your version, who would be in charge, why would that person or people be in charge? What makes your version better than Kurt Vonnegut's?

Once students finish reading the novel, they have the option to select one of the following comic strip sites to create their very own in response to the questions listed above. The comic strip sites are free; they only require users to create an account. Once students create an account, they are able to access the site.

- Bitstrips: http://www.bitstrips.com/create/comic/
- Pixton: http://pixton.com/
- Pixistrips: http://www.pikistrips.com/

If students decide they do not want to design a comic strip, they have the option to use Hypermedia to construct a critical response to the

Figure 5.1

portrayal of equality in the short story. Examples for both options are provided. The first example displays a comic strip designed by one of Brenda's students.

HYPERMEDIA

Kasha uses Hypermedia to construct a critical response to the portrayal of equality in Kurt Vonnegut's short story "Harrison Bergeron." In the story, the individual overseeing all handicaps imposed so that everyone is indeed equal, in fact as well as theory, is the United States Handicap General, Diana Moon Glampers. Kasha uses iMovie software to create a video entitled, "A Little Something on Equality" (http://www.schooltube .com/video/17483/A-little-something-on-equality), in which she presents an alternative perspective. In creating this video, she thought about the following questions:

> If you could create your own "Harrison Bergeron" story, how would you capture equality, what would equality look like in your version, who would be in charge, why would that person or those people be in charge? How would it be different from the original version?

Kasha records herself sitting in a dark room, in order to capture the Handicap General's apathy toward the people. She first explains the different types of equality—gender, racial, and social. For Kasha, the Handicap General's lack of empathy is "disturbing" and does not reflect the equality that she longs to see one day. Playing the song "*Cause a Rockslide*," by Badly Drawn Boy, she ends the video with images that capture the equality she hopes to see, in particular, equal opportunities for women. Using technology tools and resources enables Kasha to construct an alternative perspective reflecting her stance on equality.

Varied Avenues to Develop Critical Literacy Practices

Giving students varied avenues by which to develop critical literacy practices is imperative in online learning. In most cases, Brenda's students have not had a chance to openly critique texts, display their creativity, or present alternative perspectives validating their opinions. Critical literacy has not been a part of their prior learning experiences. Failure has been the only experience most of them have had. Interestingly, many students in her online class understand how to complete assignments but fail to submit them, because the assignments do not tap into their talents. They want to show what they know.

Technology tools and resources offer so many opportunities for students to develop critical literacy practices. Opportunities range from sharing an essay using Google Docs, to creating a presentation using Microsoft PowerPoint or Google Docs, to authoring hypermedia using iMovie software. (Hypermedia, as defined by Myers and Beach (2001) combines hypertext and multimedia to produce an interactive media experience.)

Therefore, as part of her pedagogy, Brenda always provides an option that allows students to use technology tools and resources to complete projects. Depending on the project, they may create a presentation, produce hypermedia, or design a comic strip.

For instance, Taylor learned a lot about himself by completing a character analysis of Sam. Through Sam, he became conscious of the ways he has shown prejudice toward others. In the end, he made a conscious effort to stop judging people based on skin color. Allowing students to make use of technology tools and resources to engage in critical literacy practices helps us achieve a paramount goal of language and literacy education: it shows them how literacy can be used as a "vehicle for social change" (Behrman 2006).

What We've Learned

Without a doubt, listening to students is the most important component of successful online teaching. By listening to her students at the beginning of the year, Brenda is able to select the most appropriate multimedia tools and resources to help them develop critical literacy practices. Providing students with many avenues for expression is also imperative in this learning environment. It encourages them to look at texts from other perspectives and produce alternative points of view. More important, it empowers her students by providing opportunities for them to find their own voice.

Works Cited

Alcott, L. M. 1982. *Little Women.* New York: Penguin.

Alvermann, D. E. 2008. "Why Bother Theorizing Adolescents' Online Literacies for Classroom Practice and Research?" *Journal of Adolescent & Adult Literacy* 52 (91): 4–6.

Alvermann, D. E., Fr. Boyd, W. Brozo, K. Hinchman, D. Moore, and E. Sturtevant. 2002. *Principled Practices for a Literate America: A Framework for Literacy and Learning in the Upper Grades:* Carnegie Corporation of New York.

Alvermann, D. E., and D. W. Moore. 1991. "Secondary School Reading." In *Handbook of Reading Research*, Vol. 2, edited by R. Barr, M. L. Kamil, P. Mosenthal, and P. D. Pearson, 951–83. New York: Longman.

Arnold, R. 1990. *Economics in Our Times.* Cincinnati, OH: West Educational.

Au, W. 2007. "High-stakes Testing and Curricular Control: A Qualitative Metasynthesis." *Educational Researcher* 36 (5): 258–67.

Ayres, K. 1998. *North by North: A Story of the Underground Railroad.* New York: Delacorte.

Barakat, I. 2007. *Tasting the Sky: A Palestinian Childhood.* New York: Farrar, Straus and Giroux.

Beach, R. 2007. *Teaching Media Literacy.com: A Web-Linked Guide to Resources and Activities.* New York: Teachers College Press.

Beach, R., and D. O'Brien. 2008. "Teaching Popular Culture Texts in the Classroom. In J. Coiro, M. Knobel, C. Lankshear, and D. J. Leu (Eds.), *Handbook of Research on New Literacies* (pp. 775–804). Mahwah, NJ: Lawrence Erlbaum.

Bean, T. W. 2002. "Text Comprehension: The Role of Activity Theory in Navigating Students' Prior Knowledge in Content Teaching." In C. Roller (Ed.), *Reading Research 2001* (pp. 133–47). Newark, DE: International Reading Association.

Bean, T. W. 2006. "*New Literacies.*" Paper presented at the annual Pearson Digital Summer Symposium, Phoenix, AZ.

Bean, T. W., S. K. Bean, and K. F. Bean. 1999. "Intergenerational Conversations and Two Adolescents' Multiple Literacies: Implications for Redefining Content Area Literacy." *Journal of Adolescent & Adult Literacy* 42 (6): 438–48.

Bean, T. W., J. E. Readence, and R. S. Baldwin. 2008. *Content Area Literacy: An Integrated Approach* (9th ed.). Dubuque, IA: Kendall/Hunt.

Bean, T., N. Walker, J. Wimmer, and B. Dillard. 2009. "How Does Creative Content Area Teaching in Cyberspace and Multimedia Settings Work with Adolescents?" In *Essential Questions in Adolescent Literacy: Teachers and Researchers Describe What Works in Classrooms*, edited by J. Lewis. New York, NY: Guilford Press.

Behrman, E. H. 2003. "Reconciling Content Literacy with Adolescent Literacy: Expanding Literacy Opportunities in a Community-Focused Biology Class." *Reading Research and Instruction* 43 (1): 1–30.

Behrman, E. 2006. "Teaching about Language, Power, and Text: A Review of Classroom Practices That Support Critical Literacy." *Journal of Adolescent & Adult Litearcy* 49 (6): 490–98.

Blaszczak, D. R. 1991. "The Roller Coaster Experiment." *American Journal of Physics* 59 (3): 283–85.

Bloor, E. 1999. *Crusader*. San Diego, CA: Harcourt Brace & Company.

Callow, J. 2008. "Show Me: Principles for Assessing Students' Visual Literacy." *The Reading Teacher* 61 (8): 616–26.

Coiro, J., and E. Dobler. 2007. "Exploring the Online Reading Comprehension Strategies Used by Sixth-Grade Skilled Readers to Search for and Locate Information on the Internet. *Reading Research Quarterly* 42 (2): 214–57.

Coiro, J., M. Knobel, C. Lankshear, and D. J. Leu. 2008. *Handbook of Research on New Literacies.* Mahwah, NJ: Lawrence Erlbaum.

Conley, M. W. 2008. "Cognitive Strategy Instruction: What We Know About the Promise, What We Don't Know About the Potential." *Harvard Educational Review* 78 (1): 84–106.

Cooney, C. B. 2005. *Code Orange.* New York: Delacorte Press.

Denenberg, B. 1997. *So Far from Home: The Diary of Mary Driscoll, an Irish Mill Girl.* New York: Scholastic.

Draper, S. 1994. *Tears of a Tiger.* New York: Aladdin Books

Dupin-Bryant, P., and B. DuCharme-Hansen. 2005. "Assessing Student Needs in Web-Based Distance Education." *International Journal of Instructional Technology and Distance Learning* 2 (1). http://itdl.org/Journal/Jan05/article04.htm

English, C. 2007. "Finding a Voice in a Threaded Discussion Group: Talking About Literature Online." *English Journal* 97 (1): 56–61.

Escobar, C. 1990. "Amusement Park Physics." *The Physics Teacher* 28 (7): 446–53.

Escobar, C. ed. 2001. *Amusement Park Physics.* College Park, MD: American Association of Physics Teachers.

Faber, J. E., J. D. Morris, and M. G. Lieberman. 2000. "The Effect of Note Taking on Ninth Grade Students' Comprehension." *Reading Psychology* 21: 257–70.

Fisher, D., N. Frey, and D. Lapp. 2009. "Meeting AYP in a High School: A Formative Experiment." *Journal of Adolescent & Adult Literacy* 52 (5): 386–96.

Gee, J. 2008. "Being a Lion and Being a Soldier: Learning and Games." In J. Coiro, M. Knobel, C. Lankshear, and D. J. Leu (Eds.), *Handbook of Research on New Literacies* (pp. 1023–36). Mahwah, NJ: Lawrence Erlbaum.

Gunning, T. 2002. *Creating Literacy Instruction for All Students.* New York: Allyn & Bacon.

Guthrie, J. 2004. "Teaching for Literacy Engagement." *Journal of Literacy Research* 36: 1–28.

Hakim, J. 1999. "1860–1863." In *War, Terrible War*, Book 5, 143–46. Washington, DC: Oxford University Press.

Hazen, W. A. 1999. *Everyday Life: The Frontier*. New Jersey: Good Year Books.

Hobbs, R. 2007. *Reading the Media: Media Literacy in High School English*. New York: Teachers College Press.

Holladay. 2006. "Understanding Cloning." *USA Today*. Available from http://www.usatoday.com/tech/columnist/aprilholladay/2006-05-15 -cloningx.htm

Houghton Mifflin English. 2001. Boston: Houghton Mifflin.

Houston, G. 1994. *Mountain Valor*. New York: Philomel.

Hynd, C. R. 2002. "*Using Multiple Texts to Teach Content.*" Paper presented at the North Central Regional Laboratory Annual Literacy Research Network Conference. Naperville, IL.

Hynd-Shanahan, C., J. Holschuh, and B. Hubbard. 2005. "Thinking Like a Historian: College Students' Reading of Multiple Historical Documents." *Journal of Literacy Research* 36: 141–76.

Ivey, G., and K. Broaddus. 2001. "Just Plain Reading: A Survey of What Makes Students Want to Read in Middle School Classrooms." *Journal of Adolescent & Adult Literacy* 36 (4): 350–77.

Keith, H. 1957. *Rifles for Watie*. New York: Harper Collins.

Kennedy, K. 2003. "Writing with Web Logs." *Technology & Learning* 23: 11–12.

Kist, W. 2002. "Finding 'New Literacy' in Action: An Interdisciplinary High School Western Civilization." *Journal of Adolescent & Adult Literacy* 45 (5): 368–77.

Kist, W. 2005. *New Literacies in Action: Teaching and Learning in Multiple Media*. New York: Teachers College Press.

Knobel, M., and C. Lankshear. 2007. *A New Literacies Sampler*. New York: Peter Lang.

Kress, G. 2003. *Literacy in the New Media Age.* London: Routledge.

Lankshear, C., and M. Knobel. 2003. *New Literacies: Changing Knowledge and Classroom Learning.* Philadelphia: Open University Press.

Lenart, A., and M. Madden. 2005. *Teen Content Creators and Consumers.* Washington, D.C.: Pew Internet & American Life Project, November 2. Available online at http://www.pewInternet.org/PPF?r?166?report_display.asp

Leu, D. J., D. D. Leu, and J. Coiro. 2004. *Teaching with the Internet, K–12: New Literacies for New Times.* Norwood, MA: Christopher-Gordon.

Lewis, B. 1990. "The Roots of Muslim Rage." *The Atlantic.* Available at www.theatlantic.com/doc/199009/muslim-rage.

Lewis. C. 2007. "New Literacies." In M. Knobel and C. Lankshear (Eds.), *A New Literacies Sampler,* 229–37. New York: Peter Lang.

McLynn, F. 1994. "Famous Letters: Messages and Thoughts That Shaped Our World." *Readers' Digest.*

McNabb, M. L. 2006. *Literacy Learning in Networked Classrooms: Using the Internet with Middle-Level Students.* Newark, DE: International Reading Association.

Myers, J., and R. Beach. 2001. "Hypermedia Authoring as Critical Literacy." *Journal of Adolescent & Adult Literacy* 44 (6): 538–46.

Moje, E. B. 2008. "Foregrounding the Disciplines in Secondary Literacy Teaching and Learning: A Call for Change." *Journal of Adolescent & Adult Literacy* 52 (2): 96–107.

Moje, E. B., M. Overby, N. Tysvaer, and K. Morris. 2008. "The Complex World of Adolescent Literacy: Myths, Motivations, and Mysteries." *Harvard Educational Review* 78 (1): 107–54.

Moore, D. W., T. W. Bean, D. Birdyshaw, and J. Rycik. 1999. "Adolescent Literacy: A Position Statement." *Journal of Adolescent & Adult Literacy* 43: 97–110.

Moorman, G., and J. Horton. 2007. "Millenials and How to Teach Them." In *Adolescent Literacy Instruction: Policies and Promising Practices,* edited by J. Lewis and G. Moorman, 263–85. Newark, DE: International Reading Association.

Morrison, T. G., J. S. Jacobs, and W. R. Swinyard. 1999. "Do Teachers Who Read Personally Use Recommended Literacy Practices in Their Classrooms?" *Reading Research and Instruction* 38 (2): 81–100.

Munoz, Ryan P. 2000. *Esperanza Rising*. New York: Scholastic.

New London Group. 1996. "A Pedagogy of Multiliteracies: Designing Social Futures." *Harvard Educational Review* 66: 60–92.

Norman, D. A. 2004. *Emotional Design: Why We Love (or Hate) Everyday Things*. New York: Basic Books.

O'Brien. D. G. 1998. "Multiple Literacies in a High-School Program for At-Risk Adolescents." In D. E. Alvermann, K. A. Hinchman, D. W. Moore, S. F. Phelps, and D. R. Waff (Eds.), *Reconceptualizing the Literacies in Adolescents' Lives*, 27–50. Mahwah, NJ: Erlbaum.

O'Brien, D. G. March 2003. "Juxtaposing Traditional and Intermedial Literacies to Redefine the Competence of Struggling Adolescents." *Reading Online*. Online journal of the International Reading Association. http://readingonline.org/newliteracies/obrien1/

O'Brien, D. 2007. "Struggling" Adolescents' Engagement in Multimediating: Countering the Institutional Construction of Incompetence." In D. E. Alvermann, K. A. Hinchman, D. W. Moore, S. F. Phelps, and D. R. Waff (Eds.), *Reconceptualizing the Literacies in Adolescents' Lives*, 2nd ed., 29–46. Mahwah, NJ: Lawrence Erlbaum.

O'Brien, D., and C. Scharber. 2008a. "Digital Literacies." *Journal of Adolescent & Adult Literacy* (September). Available at www.reading.org.

O'Brien, D., and C. Scharber. 2008b. "Digital Literacies Go to School: Potholes and Possibilities." *Journal of Adolescent & Adult Literacy* 52 (1): 66–68.

Pahl, K., and J. Rowsell. 2005. *Literacy and Education: Understanding the New Literacy Studies in the Classroom*. London: Paul Chapman.

PBS video, *The Great War and the Shaping of the 20th Century*. Available from http://www.pbs.org/greatwars/.

Pearson, P. D. July 1985b. "The Triple Read Method for Expository Text." Seminar presentation, Eastern Montana College, Billings, MT.

Phelps, S. F. 1998. "Adolescdents and Their Multiple Literacies." In D. E. Alvermann, K. A. Hinchman, D. W. Moore, S. F. Phelps, and D. R. Waff

When Textbooks Fall Short

(Eds.), *Reconceptualizing the Literacies in Adolescents' Lives* (p. 2). Mahway, NJ: Erlbaum.

Pinkney, A. D. 2001. *Silent Thunder*. New York: Hyperion.

Pressley, M. 2000. "What Should Comprehension Instruction Be the Instruction Of?" In *Handbook of Reading Research,* Vol. 3, edited by M. Kamil, P. Mosenthal, P. D. Pearson, and R. Barr. Mahweh, NJ: Lawrence Erlbaum Associates.

Readence, J. E., T. W. Bean, and R. W. Baldwin. 2004. *Content Area Literacy: An Integrated Approach* (8th ed.). Dubuque, IA: Kendall Hunt.

Rinaldi, A. 1988. *The Last Silk Dress*. New York: Holiday House.

Rinaldi, A. 1995. *Amelia's War*. New York: Scholastic.

Rooks, G. 1991. *The Non-Stop Discussion Workbook*. London: Newberry House.

Sears, S. W. 1989. *The Civil War Papers of George B. McClellan*. New York: Tickner & Fields.

Shanahan, T., and C. Shanahan. 2008. "Teaching Disciplinary Literacy to Adolescents: Rethinking Content Area Literacy." *Harvard Educational Review* 78 (1): 40–59.

Shanahan-Hynd, C. 2004. "Teaching Science Through Literacy." In T. L. Jetton and J. A. Dole (Eds.), *Adolescent Literacy Research and Practice* (75–93). New York: The Guilford Press.

Sheridan-Thomas, H. K. 2007. "Making Sense of Multiple Literacies: Exploring Pre-Service Content Area Teachers' Understanding and Applications." *Reading Research and Instruction* 46 (2): 121–47.

Smith, M. W., and J. D. Wilhelm. 2002. *"Reading Don't Fix No Chevys": Literacy in the Lives of Young Men*. Portsmouth, NH: Heinemann.

Speers, R. R. 1991. "Physics and Roller Coasters: The Blue Streak at Cedar Point." *American Journal of Physics* 59 (6): 528–33.

Speers, R. 1992. "Perspectives on the World's Tallest Roller Coaster." *The Physics Teacher* 30 (4): 216–17.

Squire, K. D. 2008. "Video-Game Literacy: A Literacy of Expertise." In J. Coiro, M. Knobel, C. Lankshear, and D. J. Leu (Eds.), *Handbook of Research on New Literacies* (635–69). Mahwah, NJ: Lawrence Erlbaum.

Stahl, S. A., and C. Shanahan. 2004. "Learning to Think Like a Historian: Disciplinary Knowledge Through a Critical Analysis of Multiple Documents." In T. L. Jetton and J. A. Dole (Eds.), *Adolescent Literacy Research and Practice* (94–115). New York: The Guilford Press.

Steinbeck, J. 1937/2006. *Of Mice and Men.* New York: Penguin.

Steinkuehler, C. A. 2008. "Cognition and Literacy in Massively Multiplayer Online Games." In J. Coiro, M. Knobel, C. Lankshear, and D. J. Leu (Eds.), *Handbook of Research on New Literacies* (611–34). Mahwah, NJ: Lawrence Erlbaum.

Stevens, L. P., and T. W. Bean. 2007. *Critical Literacy: Context, Research, and Practice in the K–12 Classroom.* Thousand Oaks, CA: SAGE.

Stone, J. C. 2007. "Popular Websites in Adolescents' Out-of-School Lives: Critical Lessons on Literacy." In *A New Literacies Sampler,* edited by M. Knobel and C. Lankshear, 49–63. New York: Peter Lang.

Tanner, R. R. 1997. "Roller Coaster Design Project." *The Physics Teacher* 35 (3): 148–49.

Tapscott, D., and A. D. Williams. 2008. *Wikinomics: How Mall Collaboration Changes Everything.* New York: Portfolio.

Thorne, S. L. 2008. "Mediating Technologies and Second Language Learning." In *Handbook of Research on New Literacies,* edited by J. Coiro, M. Knobel, C. Lankshear, and D. Leu. New York: Lawrence Erlbaum.

van Leeuwen, T. 2005. *Introducing Social Semiotics.* London, UK: Routledge.

Vonnegut, K. 2005. *Harrison Bergeron.* Retrieved September 15, 2008 from West Valley College Philosophy: http://instruct.westvalley.edu/lafave/hb.html

Wade, S. E., and E. B. Moje. 2000. "The Role of Text in Classroom Learning." In M. L. Kamil, P. B. Mosenthal, P. D. Pearson, and R. Barr (Eds.), *Handbook of Reading Research: Volume III.* Mahwah, NJ: Lawrence Erlbaum.

Walker, N. T., T. W. Bean, and B. Dillard. 2005. "Sociocultural Dimensions of Multiple Texts in Two Experienced Teachers' Classrooms." In B. Maloch, J. V. Hoffman, D. L. Schallert, C. M. Fairbanks, and J. Worthy

(Eds.), *54th Yearbook of the National Reading Conference*, 416–27. Oak Creek, WI: National Reading Conference.

Walker, N. T., and W. Bean. 2004. "Using Multiple Texts in Content Area Classrooms." *Journal of Content Area Reading* 3 (1): 23–35.

West, K. C. 2008. "Weblogs and Literacy Response: Socially Situated Identities and Hybrid Social Languages in English Class Blogs." *Journal of Adolescent & Adult Literacy* 51 (7): 588–98.

Wilder, P., and M. Dressman. 2006. "New Literacies, Enduring Challenges? The Influence of Capital on Adolescent Readers' Internet Practices." In D. E. Alvermann, K. A. Hinchman, D. W. Moore, S. F. Phelps, and D. R. Waff (Eds.), *Reconceptualizing the Literacies in Adolescents' Lives*, pp. 205–29. Mahwah, NJ: Lawrence Erlbaum.

Wilder, P., and M. Dressman. 2007. "New Literacies, Enduring Challenges? The Influence of Capital on Adolescent Readers' Internet Practices." In D. E. Alvermann, K. A. Hinchman, D. W. Moore, S. F. Phelps, and D. R. Waff (Eds.), *Reconceptualizing the Literacies in Adolescents' Lives* (2nd ed.), 205–29. Mahwah, NJ: Lawrence Erlbaum.

Winter, J. M., and B. Baggett. 1996. *1914–18: The Great War and the Shaping of the 20th Century.* London: BBC Books.

Witte, S. 2007. "That's Online Writing, Not Boring School Writing": Writing with Blogs and the Talkback Project. *Journal of Adolescent & Adult Literacy* 51 (2): 92–96.

Zucker, A., and R. Kozma. 2003. *The Virtual High School.* New York: Teachers College Press.